*do it* **NOW** *do it* **FAST** *do it* **RIGHT**™

# Paint
## Transformations

*do it* **NOW** *do it* **FAST** *do it* **RIGHT**™

# Paint
## Transformations

The Taunton Press

The Taunton Press
Inspiration for hands-on living®

The Taunton Press, Inc., 63 South Main Street, PO Box 5506, Newtown, CT 06470-5506

e-mail: tp@taunton.com

Distributed by Publishers Group West

WRITER AND PROJECT MANAGER: Roy Barnhart

SERIES EDITOR: Tim Snyder

SERIES DESIGN AND LAYOUT: Lori Wendin

ILLUSTRATOR: Melanie Powell

COVER PHOTOGRAPHERS: (front cover) all photos © Randy O'Rourke, except (from far left top) middle and bottom © David Bravo; (back cover) all photos © Randy O'Rourke, except (bottom row) third from left and far right © David Bravo

Taunton's Do It Now/Do It Fast/Do It Right™ is a trademark of
The Taunton Press, Inc., registered in the U.S. Patent and Trademark Office.

LIBRARY OF CONGRESS CATALOGING-IN-PUBLICATION DATA
Paint transformations.
        p. cm. -- (Do it now/do it fast/do it right)
Includes bibliographical references and index.
  ISBN 1-56158-670-6
  1. House painting. 2. Furniture painting. I. Taunton Press. II.
Series.
TT323.P319 2004
698'.14--dc22
                            2003022766

Printed in the United States of America
10 9 8 7 6 5 4 3 2 1

The following manufacturers/names appearing in *Paint Transformations* are trademarks: Behr® PREMIUM PLUS®; ColorSmart™; Cover-Stain®; DAP®; Dynaflex 230®; Homax®; Makita®; McCloskey®; Minwax®; Benjamin Moore®; Benjamin Moore Fresh Start®; Moore's® Alkyd Glazing Liquid; Phillips®; Pittsburgh Paints®; Scotch®; Sheetrock®; Sherwin-Williams®; Starrett Tools®; 3M®; Wagner®; Zinsser®.

# Acknowledgments

We're grateful to the contractors, design consultants, and experts whose talent and hard work helped make this book possible. Thanks to Doug Nelson, Jeanne Bracken, Susan Gardella, Diana Baxter, Sandy Harchkins, Gwendolyn Noto, Jennifer Peters, Jason Renjilian, Janice Sopata, Sarah Snyder, and Kimberly Wise. Thanks also to the Sherwin-Williams and Local Color paint stores in Fairfield, Connecticut, and to Klaff's Inc. of South Norwalk, Connecticut.

# Contents

**PAINTING PROJECTS**

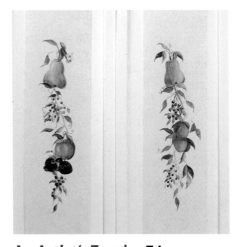

# How to Use This Book

I F YOU'RE INTERESTED IN HOME IMPROVEMENTS that add value and convenience while enabling you to express your own sense of style, you've come to the right place. **Do It Now/Do It Fast/Do It Right** books are created with an attitude that says "Let's get started!" and an ideal mix of home improvement inspiration and how-to information. Do It Now books don't skip important steps or force you to guess at what needs to be done to take a project from start to finish.

You'll find that this book has a friendly, easy-to-use format. (See the sample pages shown here.) You'll begin each project knowing exactly what tools and gear you'll need and what materials to buy at your home center or building supply outlet. You can get started confidently because every step is illustrated and explained. Along the way, you'll discover plenty of expert advice packed into the margins. For ideas on how to personalize your project, check out the design options pages that follow the step-by-step instructions.

## WORK TOGETHER

If you like company when you go to the movies or clean up the kitchen, you'll probably feel the same way about tackling home improvement projects. The work will go faster, and you'll have a partner to share in the adventure. You'll

Get the TOOLS & GEAR you need. You'll also find out what features and details are important.

DO IT FAST saves you time and trouble.

LINGO explains words that the pros know.

DO IT RIGHT tells you what it takes to get topnotch results.

Know exactly WHAT TO BUY. This list of materials and project supplies will get you in and out of the home center without wasting time.

COOL TOOL puts you in touch with tools that make the job easier.

see that some projects really call for another set of hands to help hold parts in place or steady a ladder. Read through the project you'd like to tackle and note where you're most likely to need help.

## PLANNING AND PRACTICE PAY OFF

Most of the projects in this book can easily be completed in a weekend. But the job can take longer if you don't pay attention to planning and project preparation requirements. Check out the conditions in the area where you'll be working. Sometimes repairs are required before you can begin to build or install your project. For help, check out the basic techniques in Prep Projects (p. 14). Get Set (p. 4) will tell you about the tools and materials required for most of the projects in this book.

Your skill and confidence will improve with every project you complete. But if you're trying a technique for the first time, it's wise to rehearse before you "go live." This means ordering a little extra in the way of supplies and materials and finding a location where you can practice your technique.

**DESIGN OPTIONS** Complete your project with different dimensions, finishes, and details. Explore design options to personalize your project.

**DO IT RIGHT** tells you what it takes to get top-notch results.

**WHAT CAN GO WRONG** explains how to avoid common mistakes.

**STEP-BY-STEP** pages get you started and keep you going to finish the job.

# Get Set

Collect the right ingredients for paint projects so you can
**DO IT NOW, DO IT FAST** & **DO IT RIGHT**

IF YOU LOVE THE WAY THAT PAINT can transform a room but dread the mess and the obstacles you need to overcome to get started, you've come to the right place. This kickoff chapter will get you set to take on any painting project quickly and confidently. There's a bit about everything here—from selecting a color scheme and controlling the mess, to collecting the tools you need and choosing compatible, top-quality

primers and top coats. Armed with this information, you'll be able to get exactly what you need from the home center or paint store, get to work without wasting time, and enjoy the adventure of re-creating a room with your own sense of style.

✦ DO IT NOW

**Save money on samples.** Your paint dealer can supply you with small cans of the colors you're curious about. There's no need to buy a gallon.

# Color Comes First

**COLOR IS WHAT GETS US EXCITED** about paint projects, but choosing paint colors can be a challenge. It's intimidating to find the "perfect" color when your choices are limitless. The good news is that you won't have any trouble finding expert help at home centers and paint suppliers. Follow these guidelines and bring your questions to your paint dealer.

**TRY BEFORE YOU BUY.** The color samples that paint manufacturers make available are free and helpful. But to truly test out your color choices, it's best to either buy a small can of paint and apply it to an area, or make up a large sample board (on a piece of drywall or poster board) and put it in place on the wall or ceiling. Then step back and evaluate the results.

**PAY ATTENTION TO LIGHT & LIGHTING.** Natural and artificial light both affect color. Before finalizing your color decisions, make sure you have a chance to view your choices under the different lighting conditions that will prevail in the room.

**LET FURNISHINGS DRIVE THE DECISION.** Sometimes your color choices need to revolve around a favorite piece of furniture, special painting, or unique rug. When furnishings are the focal point in a room, use their colors to inspire your choices for walls, ceilings, and trim.

**TRY SOME VIRTUAL PAINTING.** Online tools such as Personal Color Viewer (www.benjaminmoore.com) or ColorSmart™ (www.behrpaint.com) can help you narrow your color choices or identify appealing color schemes by allowing you to "paint" a sample room.

## WHAT'S YOUR THEME?

Paint gives you a nearly instant way to reinvent a room. It's also a great way to express your sense of style. If you're daunted by all of the colors, combinations, and decorative effects that are possible, it helps to identify a theme and plan your painting project around it. Here are a few common themes to get you started on your painting adventure.

**BOLD COLORS FOR SMALL SPACES.** Half bathrooms, kids' rooms, laundry rooms, and utility rooms are all

*Match the mood of the room with the colors you choose. In a bedroom that usually means using pastels, which are soft, pale versions of virtually any color.*

great candidates for bold, bright paint jobs. Bright colors (especially greens, yellows, and reds) and dramatic color contrasts (between walls, ceiling, trim, and furnishings) give these smaller rooms big identities. Bold and bright colors can also give you energy for mundane tasks in laundry and utility rooms. Try it, you'll like it.

**BE FORMAL.** If you entertain, you can use color to distinguish the public spaces in your home from the private ones. Blue and other cool colors do a great job of creating a more formal mood, which might be desirable in an entry foyer or dining room.

**TAKE IT EASY.** To promote a calm, relaxed mood in a study or bedroom, tone down your hues and avoid high contrasts. Light hues of just about any color will work.

**SHOW OFF WITH NEUTRALS.** This strategy works if you've got colorful paintings, interesting furniture, and beautiful furnishings to show off. You want your wall and ceiling colors to whisper instead of shout, so look at white and light brown hues.

**Getting set to paint** usually involves more than basic gear like brushes, rollers, and drop cloths. With a few extra items, you'll have what it takes to complete common repairs and prep projects. Consider adding these tools and materials to your toolbox:

**TOOLS**
• Multitip screwdriver
• Caulking gun
• Putty knife
• 5-in-1 tool
• Utility knife

**MATERIALS**
• Disposable gloves
• Joint tape (paper & fiberglass mesh)
• Joint compound
• Sandpaper (120 grit)
• White acrylic caulk

# Getting Organized

**PAINTING IS EASIER** and more fun when you've got a place to keep your gear. A work station like the one shown on p. 5 is easy to set up along a garage, basement, or utility room wall. Paint cans, roller trays, drop cloths, and other large items can fit on a countertop or on some wide shelves. Brushes, rollers, putty knives, and other tools are all hang-up items. Attach some wood strips or pegboard to the wall and buy a supply of hooks, hangers, and long finish nails so you can keep these tools in order.

## 10 TIPS FOR CONTROLLING THE MESS

**1 | MASK WITH PAINTER'S TAPE.** This tape comes in different widths and different levels of tack, or stickiness. Have a good selection of tape on hand, and use it to mask areas adjacent to those that will be painted. Painter's tape can also cover electrical switches and outlets.

**2 | PROTECT FLOORS WITH CANVAS DROP CLOTHS.** Canvas is best on the floor because (unlike plastic) it absorbs paint drips so they don't get transferred to your shoes. Protect carpet with a double layer of canvas.

**3 | MOVE WHAT YOU CAN, COVER WHAT YOU CAN'T.** Remove everything you can from the room. As for the big stuff that needs to stay, move it to the center of the room and cover it with painter's plastic—thin, inexpensive sheeting that comes on a roll. You can also use painter's plastic to cover chandeliers and other fixtures.

**4 | USE PLASTIC PAINT BUCKETS.** When brushing, don't apply paint straight from the paint can, especially if the can is full. Instead, pour a manageable amount of paint into a plastic paint bucket. These inexpensive containers are easier to handle and very easy to clean and reuse.

**5 | DRESS FOR A MESS.** Old clothes that fit comfortably are best. You'll also want to wear a painter's hat (ask for one where you buy your paint) and protective eyewear when painting overhead.

**6 | ISOLATE THE ROOM.** Control traffic into and out of the room where you're painting. Only one doorway or opening needs to be used.

**7 | USE A BOX FAN TO EXHAUST SANDING DUST.** If you have to sand trim or wallboard surfaces, use a box fan to blow dust-laden air outdoors (see the drawing below). By increasing air circulation, a fan also helps to get paint fumes out of the house.

**8 | AVOID OVERLOADING.** Trying to carry too much paint on your roller or brush can lead to dripping disasters. Get a feel for how much finish you can get on your roller or brush without causing big drips or roller spray and stick with this amount.

**9 | KEEP A RAG IN YOUR BACK POCKET.** It's important to wipe up spills right away.

**10 | HAVE A CLEANUP PLAN.** Before you begin to paint, clear the sink of dirty dishes and know where your rags and paper towels are. Set up a paint work station (see p. 5) to keep your supplies and gear organized. Finally, always leave enough time for cleaning brushes and your work area.

*Mix and pour paints in an out-of-the-way area where accidents don't become disasters.*

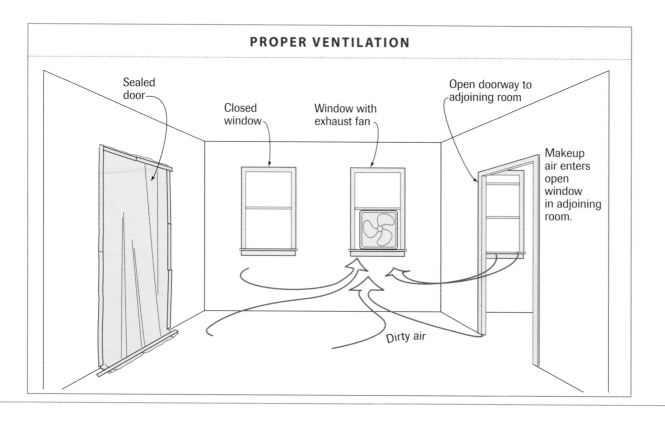

**PROPER VENTILATION**

Sealed door

Closed window

Window with exhaust fan

Open doorway to adjoining room

Makeup air enters open window in adjoining room.

Dirty air

## ▶ LINGO

**What's bad for hair is good for bristles. The split ends on a good-quality paintbrush are called flagged ends, and they help the brush to carry paint and apply it smoothly. You should be able to feel and see the flagged ends on a premium brush.**

# Brushes, Rollers, Trays & Pads

**TOOLS ARE IMPORTANT.** Without good ones, the work is harder and it's difficult to get topnotch results. Here's what you need to know about the gear that gets the paint from bucket to wall.

## BRUSHES

Paintbrushes are available in many widths, but for interior work, two sizes will handle most of your projects. Buy a 1½-in.-wide brush for painting trim and details. Many painters prefer to use a **sash brush** because its angled bristles allow for more control when painting window mullions and other delicate trim. You'll also need a big brush—one that's 3½ in. or 4 in. wide. This is the tool for cutting in along the corners where walls and ceilings meet and for applying glazes. **Synthetic-bristle brushes** are best for latex paints. For oil-based (alkyd) paints, you'll need a natural-bristle brush or a synthetic-bristle brush that's recom-

mended for use with alkyd finishes. Buy the best brushes you can afford. Premium brushes are worth the extra expense; they'll last longer and enable you to get faster and better results.

## ROLLERS

To be well equipped for painting projects, it's good to have two 9-in. rollers (for large painting projects where you'll have a helper) and one 4-in. roller for narrow areas. Roller covers slip over your rollers and have dense naps designed to carry a lot of paint. Buy these covers as you need them, but always have some extras on hand. Covers with medium naps—⅜ in. or ½ in.—will handle most of your rolling work. Make sure you also have an extension pole to screw into the handle of your roller.

## OTHER APPLICATION TOOLS

Painting pads can be useful in some situations—like applying varnish on a wood floor. But pads don't hold as much paint as a good brush, and they can be prone to dripping. Talk to your paint supplier about alternative application tools that may be appropriate for certain painting projects.

## BRUSHWORK 101

Want to paint like a pro? You'll get there faster if you know how to dip, load, slap, and lap. Try out these basic techniques on your next painting project.

**DIP & LOAD.** Dip your brush only deep enough to cover about two-thirds of the bristles. This will load a good-quality brush with plenty of paint. Keeping the upper third of your bristles dry will help you avoid drips, minimize waste, and simplify brush cleaning.

**SLAP.** Don't use the edge of your paint container to drag paint off the brush. Instead, lift the bristles out of the paint and give the brush a firm slap on the side of the container. This will drive paint onto inner bristles while removing excess paint on outer bristles.

**LAP.** Hold the brush loosely, with your fingertips extending down toward the metal ferrule that helps hold the bristles in place. Bring the broad tip of the brush evenly into contact with the surface to be painted and immediately brush out in one direction. Then brush back in the opposite direction, overlapping the first paint by about ½ in. or so. To avoid lap marks, avoid brushing into just-painted areas. Instead, brush from wet to dry.

*You need a big brush to paint a room. Look for straight, dense bristles that have finely split (flagged) tips.*

## ▶ DO IT RIGHT

**To prevent unused paint** from skimming over and drying out, pour it into a smaller can and seal the lid tightly. Most paint stores have empty cans in stock that you can use to preserve your paint supply.

## ✚ COOL TOOL

**Stepladders are essential** for many painting projects, but you may be tempted to buy more ladder than you need. If your house has standard 8-ft. ceilings, a small stepladder will usually give you the elevation you need, and it's much easier to move around and store than larger models.

# Picking the Right Paint

**YOU'RE TOOLED UP** with the right brushes, rollers, drop cloths, and other gear. Now it's time to buy your paint. To get what you need without wasting time, the tips below are good to know.

**WATER-BASED PAINT IS USUALLY BEST.** Water-based paint is also known as latex or acrylic-latex paint. The best of these paints can more than match oil-based, or alkyd, paints in workability, beauty, fade-resistance, and durability. Plus you get to clean up with soap and water instead of with solvent. Unless your paint dealer tells you otherwise, your best bet is to go with water-based paint. The best water-based paints usually contain 100% acrylic resins, so look for this description on the can.

**CUSTOM COLORS ARE NO PROBLEM.** Paint is manufactured in standard colors, but your paint dealer has the equipment to mix a custom color quickly and easily. Just bring in a sample of the color you want.

**PRIMERS ARE IMPORTANT.** Primers are formulated differently than top coats because their main job is to seal and bond. Make sure to buy a primer that is recommended for the job you have planned. Some primers are best suited for use on drywall or plaster, while others are best on bare wood or trim that has been stained or varnished. Ask your paint dealer what primer is best for the project you're planning.

**YOU USUALLY GET WHAT YOU PAY FOR.** Premium-quality paint is a pleasure to apply because of how easily it flows off the brush or roller. Because premium pigments are used, quality paint is more durable than cheaper stuff. It also dries to a smoother, more uniform finish. Manufacturers have to pay more for top-quality ingredients, so they charge more for premium paint.

**FLAT IS FOR WALLS; SEMIGLOSS IS FOR TRIM.** We're talking about sheen here—a measure of how shiny the finish will be when it dries. Paint labeled as flat or (less frequently) matte is best for use on walls and ceilings. This sheen-less finish does the

best job of hiding surface imperfections. Moving up from flat, you'll find that low-sheen finishes like eggshell and satin are often used on kitchen and bathroom walls that need more resistance to staining and moisture. Semigloss sheen is favored for trim.

**COVERAGE IS EASY TO CALCULATE.** The square footage you can expect a can of paint to cover is listed on the label. But keep in mind that rough, porous surfaces absorb more paint than smooth ones. To calculate coverage requirements for painting the walls and ceiling of a room, add the combined areas of each wall to the ceiling area, then subtract the space taken up by windows and doorways. Remember to double your coverage if you anticipate applying two coats.

## SAFE & LEGAL CLEANUP

You can find out about disposing of unused paint by checking with the local branch of the Environmental Protection Agency. In many cases, water-based paints must be allowed to dry hard before they can be added to your regular trash. Alkyd/oil-based paints are considered toxic and should be brought to a site that collects such materials.

*The primer you use depends on the surface and the type of paint you apply over it. Ask your dealer to recommend a primer that matches your project and the top coat you plan to use.*

# Prep Projects

**PATCH** holes small and large, **FIX** popped nails, **FILL** cracks
**& REMOVE** wallpaper

I T'S TRUE THAT PAINT OFTEN accentuates imperfections, so preparation is key to a great looking paint job. Start with a thorough vacuuming to get rid of cobwebs and dust on the tops of trim and on the sills. Remove scuff marks with a spray cleaner and sponge or a kitchen scrubbie and a little powdered cleanser. Wash trim with a mild detergent/water solution. Mildew must be killed, or it will reappear. Apply a 1:3 laundry bleach–water solution with a sprayer or sponge, let it sit for 15 minutes, and rinse it well with water or a vinegar-water solution. On kitchen grease use a detergent/water solution.

Fill minor imperfections, such as picture hook holes, with fast-drying spackling compound. More involved repairs are described on the following pages.

| PATCH HOLES | FIX NAIL POPS | REPAIR CRACKS | REMOVE WALLPAPER |

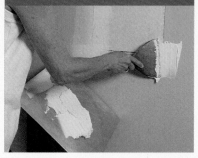

# Patch Holes

**1** **PREPARE TO PATCH.** Use a utility knife to cut a patch piece of drywall. Score along the cut line, then fold and cut all the way through from the opposite side. Hold the patch over the damaged wall area and trace its perimeter. Cut along your marks using a drywall saw.

**2** **INSTALL THE PATCH.** Cut two pieces of scrap lumber, such as plywood or a strip of wood, so they are at least 6 in. longer than the opening height. Attach these pieces with two 1¼-in. drywall screws at each end. Then secure the drywall to the nailers with screws at each corner.

**3** **TAPE & MUD.** Apply self-adhering, fiberglass-mesh joint tape over the joints, smoothing it with a taping knife. Working from a supply of joint compound on a hawk (shown) or in a bread pan, use a taping knife to apply the "mud" and then smooth the compound over

the tape. Scrape the compound off the knife on the edge of the hawk (or pan) after each smoothing pass. Allow the compound to dry completely between coats (it turns bright white).

**4** **APPLY TWO ADDITIONAL COATS OF COMPOUND.** Extend each application past the previous coat. If available, use a wider knife for the third coat. Although sanding is typically done only after the final coat, sand the second coat lightly if it dries rough or uneven. If you do sand, brush off the dust before applying the next coat.

**5** **SAND & PRIME.** Use a rubber sanding block and 120-grit sandpaper to smooth the repair. Sand until you can no longer see or feel any ridges at the outer edges, but avoid sanding into the paper facing, as it will become fuzzy. If necessary apply another very thin coat to fill pinholes, scratches, or fuzz. Vacuum off the dust and apply your primer.

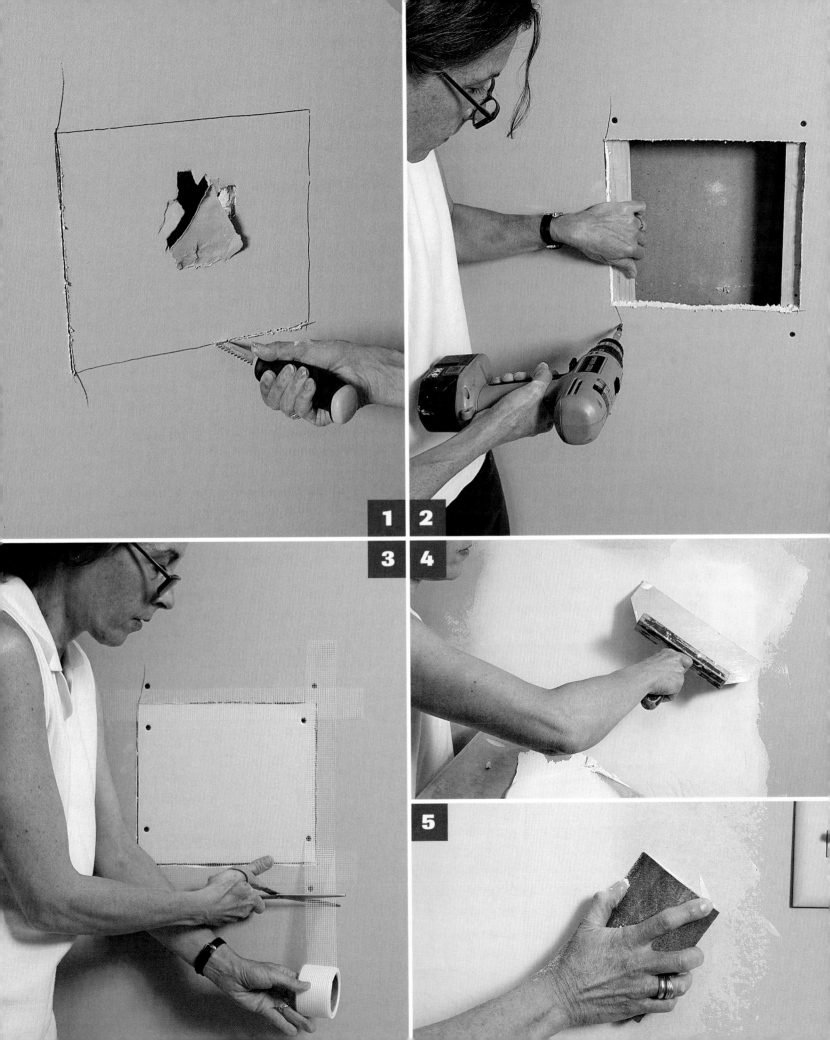

**1**

**2**

**3**

**4**

**5**

# Fix Nail Pops & Loose Corner Beads

**1** **SECURE DRYWALL AT THE NAIL POP.** Use two 1⅝-in. drywall screws. Press firmly to hold the drywall tight as you drive the screws until the heads are just below the surface but not through the paper facing. Then hammer the popped fastener below the surface. Cut away any damaged or delaminated paper facing and apply three coats of compound (see p. 16).

**2** **SECURE LOOSE CORNER BEAD.** Drive one or more screws, making sure each screw head is just below the surface. (Tip: To make sure it's below the surface, draw a taping knife across the surface—you should not hear a metallic "click" as the blade passes over the screw.) Cut away any loose material, apply joint tape, and finish as described below.

# Repair Cracks

**1** **FILL FINE CRACKS.** Apply painter's caulk with a caulking gun, then smooth the caulk with a wet finger. Repair larger cracks (such as those over doorways) with tape and drywall compound, as shown on p. 16.

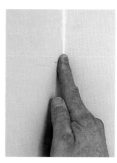

**2** **TAPE LARGER CRACKS.** Scrape the crack with a 5-in-1 tool or screwdriver to make sure nothing sticks up above the surface and that there are no loose fragments. Apply a bedding coat of fast-drying lightweight compound and press on a piece of paper joint tape. (If you use fiberglass-mesh tape, smooth it in place over the crack before applying any compound.) Apply second and third coats as necessary.

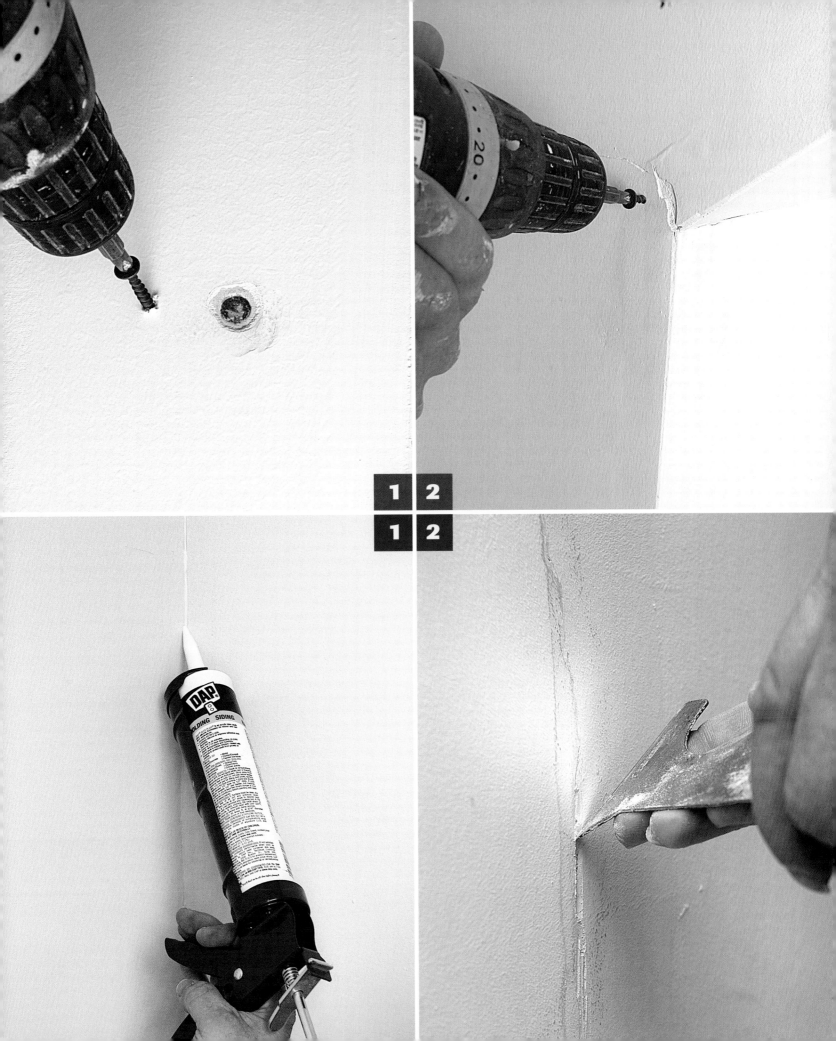

# Remove Wallpaper

**1** **PEEL OFF THE DECORATIVE LAYER.** Get under the top corner with a taping or putty knife and peel it off across the top. Then roll the paper onto a dowel or cardboard tube and roll the tube down the wall. For vinyl-coated paper, use a special perforating tool (see COOL TOOL, left) or scrape a saw down the wall to penetrate surface so the wallpaper remover can soak in.

**2** **SPRAY ON SOME WALLPAPER REMOVER.** This solution needs to soak through the paper to dissolve the wallpaper adhesive. Wipe the surface with a latex-gloved hand to distribute remover evenly...and then wait.

**3** **SCRAPE OFF THE WET PAPER.** Use a wallpaper scraper to remove the paper. Regular wallpaper should scrape off after a few minutes. Vinyl-coated paper can take an hour or more and require repeated applications of remover. Work carefully and patiently to avoid damaging the wall.

**4** **USE A WALLPAPER STEAMER.** If wallpaper remover isn't working well, try steaming stubborn paper off with a wallpaper steamer. To protect wood floors, adhere a 2-ft.-wide strip of plastic to the baseboard trim and cover it with absorbent toweling or other material to absorb the water that drips down the wall.

**5** **WASH OFF RESIDUE.** When all the paper is removed, wash the walls with a detergent and warm water solution. Rinse and wring out your sponge, and change the water often. You want to remove the paste, not just move it around. Use clean water for a final wipe-down.

# Painting a Room

**A fresh COAT OF COLOR gives any room a new personality**

P AINTING A ROOM HAS THE SAME FEEL-GOOD POTENTIAL as shopping for new clothes. There's plenty of excitement about choosing the right color combinations and about the way you're going to feel when you're done.

Like other paint projects, this is one that can be done solo. But it's faster and more fun with two people. In terms of planning, you'll need to decide if you want to paint the trim as well as the walls and ceiling. It's best to get trim, doors, and windows painted before you begin to paint the ceiling and walls (see p. 34).

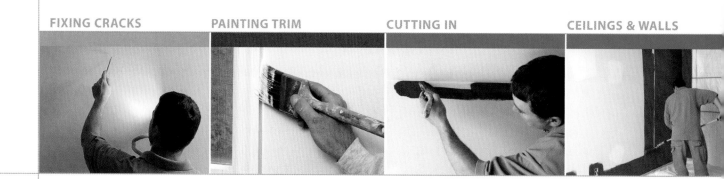

FIXING CRACKS  PAINTING TRIM  CUTTING IN  CEILINGS & WALLS

▶ **DO IT RIGHT**

**Acoustic or popcorn ceiling** texture can easily be ruined by using the wrong type of paint, applying too much paint, or excessive rolling. Use oil-based paint and a long-nap roller. Or use an airless sprayer, following the manufacturer's instructions.

✦ **DO IT NOW**

**Dress for success!** Wear old sneakers, painter's pants, a long-sleeve T-shirt, and a painter's cap. When using a roller, wear goggles to protect your eyes (and eyeglasses) from paint roller-spray.

➕ **WHAT CAN GO WRONG**

**A new roller can shed** some fuzz and leave it behind as you roll on your paint. To prevent this, wrap a new roller cover with masking tape. When you peel off the tape nearly all of the loose stuff comes off with the tape.

# Tools & Gear

*Painting a room can require as little as a roller and tray, a paintbrush, and a drop cloth. But with a few inexpensive extras, you'll get top-notch results. This extra gear will also make the job go faster and easier.*

**CLEANING SUPPLIES.** Wall and ceiling surfaces may be dirtier than you think, and any deposits of dust or grime can prevent paint from adhering well. For quick, thorough cleaning, you'll need a vacuum, sponges, a bucket, rags, and a household cleaner that won't leave a soapy residue.

**REPAIR TOOLS.** Have a putty knife handy for applying spackling compound and a caulking gun for applying caulk. If repairs are more extensive than small cracks and holes, see p. 16.

**ROLLER, EXTENSION POLE & TRAY.** Each painter needs a 9-in. roller with a screw-in extension pole. If you're painting with partners, get an extra tray.

**3-IN. NYLON-POLYESTER BRUSH.** This is what you'll use to paint trim and to cut in around windows and doors and along corners.

**STEPLADDER.** You'll need a sturdy stepstool or a stepladder for repair work and painting above windows and doors.

**DROP CLOTH.** A canvas drop cloth will protect the floor where you're painting. If there's wall-to-wall carpet on the floor, put down a double layer.

**SCREWDRIVERS.** To remove door hardware and outlet covers, you'll need a screwdriver for Phillips® head and slotted screws.

# What to Buy

**1 | REPAIR SUPPLIES.** In any room, you can expect to find small cracks and holes in wall and ceiling surfaces. To repair these areas, buy some spackling compound and acrylic painter's caulk. Caulk is mainly for filling cracks between trim and wall or ceiling surfaces. Spackling compound is for other cracks and holes.

**2 | PRIMER & PAINT.** Choose an interior primer or primer/sealer compatible with the top coat you'll be using. If your top coat will be a color other than white or light tan, ask the dealer to tint the primer so that its color is similar to the color of the top coat. Choose a high-quality interior acrylic-latex paint as your wall and ceiling top coat. You can go with a standard color or have the dealer custom-tint the paint for you. You'll need to select either a flat or eggshell sheen (see Get Set, p. 12). To figure out how much you need, measure your room and record how many doors and windows you have. Someone at the paint store can then help you figure out how much paint you'll need.

**3 | ROLLER COVERS.** You'll need one for each painter. Buy thin-nap ($\frac{3}{8}$-in. or $\frac{1}{2}$-in.) covers, which are best for smooth surfaces. The best roller covers have beveled edges to minimize roller tracks.

**4 | PROTECTION.** Make sure to have a roll of painter's plastic drop cloth to cover furniture, chandeliers, and other items that need protection from paint drips. For personal protection, don't forget a painter's cap and goggles.

**5 | PAINTER'S TAPE.** Painter's masking tape is what you want. Get a $\frac{3}{4}$-in. roll and a 2-in. roll. Other masking products might also help to prevent paint spills from getting where they shouldn't. You can also buy pregummed paper or lightweight plastic drapes with tape from your paint supplier.

## WHAT CAN GO WRONG

**M**ildew can prevent paint from adhering to a surface. This mold is often found in damp locations like bathrooms, laundry rooms, or areas with little or no air circulation. **Telltale signs:** moldy smell and dark, blotchy deposits. **What to do:** Sponge or spray on a 1:1 solution of laundry bleach and water. Let stand 5 minutes, then wipe down and neutralize with water or a water-vinegar solution. Repeat if necessary.

# Cleaning & Caulking

**1** **PREPARE THE ROOM.** Clear out everything you can. Remove outlet covers and apply painter's tape over switches and receptacles. Consolidate any remaining furniture in the center of the room and protect it with plastic drop cloths. Cover the floor with canvas drop cloths. Don't forget to cover any built-in furniture and any ceiling fans.

**2** **FIND THEN FIX CRACKS & HOLES.** It's easier to discover cracks and depressions when you shine a bright light across the surface. Fill holes and cracks with spackling compound. Sand the repair area smooth after the compound dries. If you're doing a lot of sanding, put a box fan in a window to draw dust-laden air outside.

**3** **CAULK THE CRACKS.** Scrape out any cracked or dried caulk where moldings meet walls or ceilings. An old screwdriver makes a good scraping tool; a painter's 5-in-1 tool works even better. Apply a ⅛-in.-dia. bead of caulk along all trim/wall junctures that have open cracks, smooth the bead with a wetted fingertip, and allow it to skin over before painting.

**4** **PAINT THE TRIM FIRST.** If your plan is to paint walls, ceiling, and trim, then it's best to get the trim painted first, along with the room's windows and doors. (See the project that begins on p. 34.) When

you're ready to start on the ceiling and walls, mask off the trim with painter's tape or pregummed masking paper. Don't forget to protect interior window sills from roller drips. And don't forget to clean the walls and ceiling before you start painting.

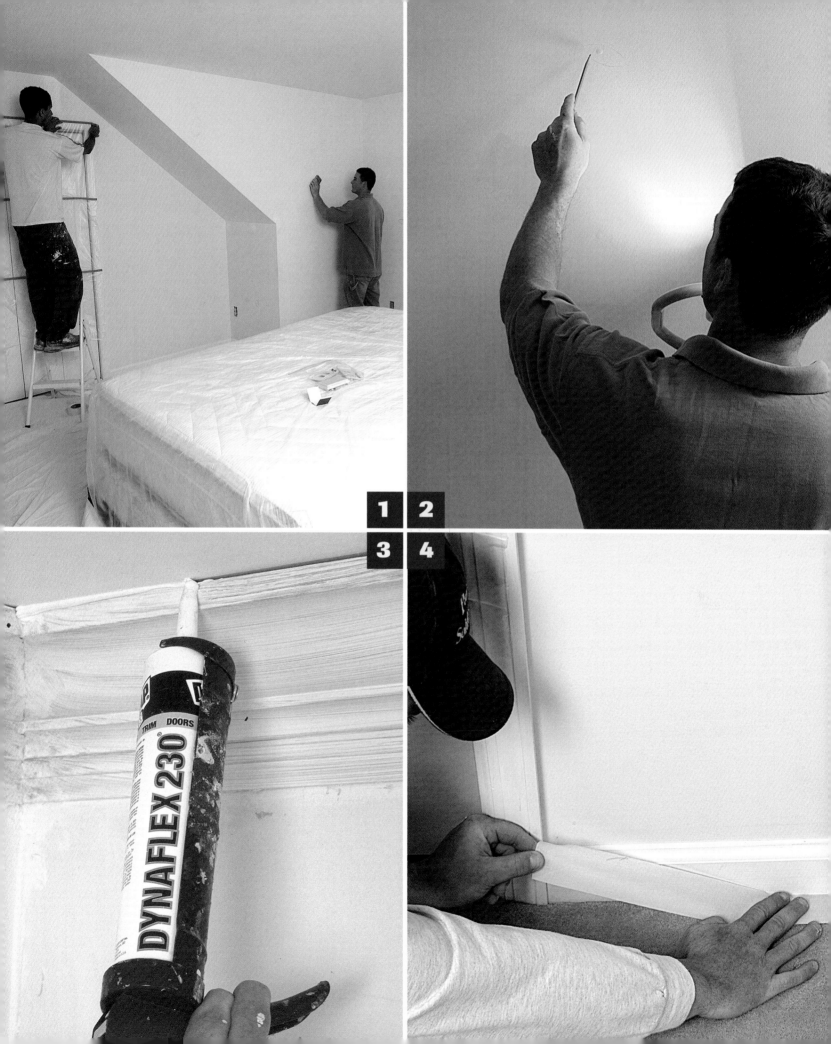

# Cutting & Rolling

**5** **CUT IN THE CEILING.** Always paint the ceiling before the walls. Using a 3-in. paintbrush, apply a band of paint on the ceiling where it meets the wall. You can cut in the ceiling all around the room or work on one section at a time. When there's a pair of painters working, one can cut in with a brush while the other begins to roll.

**6** **LET'S ROLL!** Screw the roller extension into your roller. Dip into your paint tray and roll out the paint on the tray's slanted surface until the nap is evenly coated. Begin rolling the ceiling next to the wall, where you've cut in with the brush. Then roll a big "W" pattern in an area about 3 ft. square. Fill in the open areas in the W, then move on and repeat the process.

**7** **CUT IN THE WALLS.** Use your 3-in. brush to cut in one wall at a time. Brush a band of paint down the corners, around window and door openings, and above the baseboard. If the walls are being painted a different color than the ceiling, take more care when cutting in along these corners.

**8** **ROLL THE WALLS.** Work from one end of a wall to the other. Start your roller at the top of the wall, then roll straight up and down just until you've applied an even coat. When you're finished, peel off the masking tape, clean up the room, and put away your gear. Wow! Your new room looks great.

5 6
7 8

Big color in a little space. If having fun is part of the program, a bold color will get the message across.

Orange may not be the first color that comes to mind for a bedroom, but why not? This shade looks fresh paired with white ceiling and trim—and with shades of blue, the complementary color of orange.

Green can go with any color. This shade of green leans toward red rather than yellow to give it a softness that goes well with rich orange-golds and purple-browns. White trim keeps the look of the room bright.

# Wake-up call. Builders play it safe and give most rooms the all-white or off-white treatment. If your plans are to cover the walls with bright artwork or install curtains and window treatments in contrasting colors, these highlights look good against a neutral background. But a bold color on walls and/or ceilings is still the most dramatic way to wake up a bland room. A contrasting trim color looks nice, too.

Just one color paired with white can transform a bathroom beyond the ordinary. Take a look and you'll see that white predominates, making it easier to select fixtures and accessories. Add mint-green paint and the bathroom instantly looks clean, cheery, and stylish.

You may want to balance a rich wall color with a light ceiling. This lovely red-toned dark lavender gets a lift from the white ceiling and trim and from the yellow-toned pine floorboards.

Paint can add details that don't exist in the three-dimensional world. Paint trims a round window and low doorway—and a moon—at the entrance to an understair playspace for kids. Blue paint indicates the sloped ceiling inside and so may dissuade taller folk from entering.

A pale pink would have been the choice for a serene ambience, but fuchsia walls give a bedroom a sophistication that balances the frothy bedlinens.

A classic, slate-blue color is a perfect choice for a bedroom in a traditionally styled house. The color is kept just to the wainscoting to keep the room bright, and true white trim reinforces the crisp, serene look.

# Painting Trim

To make a good room look great, transform **MOLDINGS, WINDOWS & DOORS** with fresh coats of paint

TAINED TRIM MAY BE JUST RIGHT for a cabin or lodge, where rustic seems right. But paint is the way to go if you want a room's moldings, windows, and doors to really pop. Trim colors that contrast with walls and ceilings might suit your style in one room, while a more subtle color change might be right somewhere else in the house. (For some design ideas, see p. 44.) Either way, this painting project calls for some smart prep work and a combination of tricks and proven techniques to get the pro results you want. Let's get started!

PREP STEPS          TRIM TEST          GET THE DOORS DONE          WINDOW VIEW

# Tools & Gear

**SCREWDRIVER.** A 4-in-1 driver is just the ticket for removing hardware.

**HAMMER & NAILSET.** To set trim nails, you'll need a 16-ounce hammer and a $^{1}/_{32}$-in. or $^{2}/_{32}$-in. nailset.

**PUTTY KNIFE OR 5-IN-1 TOOL.** Either tool will spackle and fill nail holes but the 5-in-1 is much more versatile. It can open paint cans, scrape out cracks, help clean your roller, and apply putty, too.

**WINDOW SCRAPER.** This small scraper is what you need for removing dried paint from window glass. Make sure you have at least a 10-pack of razor blades designed for use in the scraper.

**TAPING KNIFE.** The 5-in. taping and finishing knife has a special application unrelated to its primary purpose: It's used in combination with a window scraper to maintain a frame-to-glass seal when removing paint from windows. (See WHAT CAN GO WRONG on p. 42.)

**CAULKING GUN.** Get the kind with a quick-release button and an integral wire for breaking the seal on caulk cartridges.

**TRIM BRUSH.** If you don't have a good one, buy a new one. Size-wise, 2 in. is a good all-purpose width. Some people prefer the angled-tip over the standard. Some use both. If you need to paint wide trim (like a broad cornice molding or tall baseboard), a 3-in. brush will speed the work.

**STEPLADDER.** A necessity for reaching ceiling moldings.

## ⁕ WHAT'S DIFFERENT?

**All-purpose primers** and primer-sealers recommended for drywall and bare wood are not the best sealers to use on interior trim that has been stained and varnished. You're better off using a primer formulated for use on stained and varnished surfaces.

## ▶ DO IT RIGHT

**You know it's not a good idea** to paint yourself into a corner, but did you know that there's a painting sequence for doors and windows that will help you get better results? Here are the rules:

1 | Paint from the inside out.

2 | Paint detailed areas before flat surfaces.

3 | Paint parallel with the length or grain of wood, not across or against it.

## COOL TOOL

**W**agner® **Glass Mask system** lays down a clear masking film on a windowpane. It's spaced $^{1}/_{8}$-in. away from the frame to allow paint to extend onto the glass. This frame-to-pane seal prevents condensation or rain from getting into this joint, which causes paint failure and eventually rot. Then the tool's scraper head easily removes the film (along with any paint on it) but leaves $^{1}/_{8}$-in.-wide band of paint on the pane perimeter.

# What to Buy

**1| CAULK.** Acrylic-latex caulk is what you want. A single cartridge will be more than enough for a room.

**2| WOOD PUTTY OR PATCHING COMPOUND.** To be sure you're getting the right goop, read the label and product description. Look for the words "non-shrinking" and "fast-drying."

**3| ABRASIVES & DEGLOSSER.** 120-grit aluminum oxide sandpaper will do a good job of scuffing up the surface of varnish or semigloss paint. Half-a-dozen 9x11 sheets will handle an average-size room. Deglosser, also called liquid sandpaper, does a chemical scuff-up on varnished surfaces. Use this if your trim is ornately contoured (difficult to sand) or coated with high-gloss varnish. Deglosser is available where paint is sold.

**4| PAINTER'S TAPE.** Depending on your circumstances you may need low-tack painter's tape for freshly painted or wallpapered walls, medium-tack painter's tape for floors and any hardware, and regular high-tack masking tape for carpeting.

**5| PRIMER-SEALER.** When repairs or sanding exposes raw wood, a primer-sealer compatible with the top coat provides the base paint needed for a good bond. Painting over stained or varnished trim? Use a stain-killing, bonding primer. Primer can be tinted to approximate trim color.

**6| PAINT.** Buy a good-quality semigloss trim paint. Latex paint will be fine for most trimwork; look for the words "100% acrylic" on the label.

**7| PAINT BUCKETS.** Plastic paint buckets are inexpensive and allow you to carry around just the right amount of paint.

**8| OTHER STUFF.** Have plenty of clean rags on hand. If your paint store has them in stock, a plastic paint-can spout makes it easier to avoid drips when you pour paint from the can.

---

## SASHES FIRST, THEN JAMBS

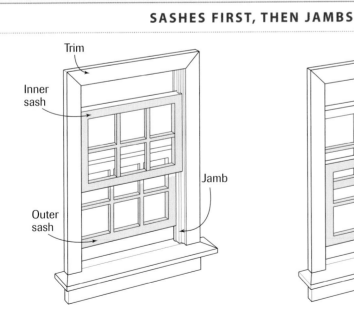

- Trim
- Inner sash
- Jamb
- Outer sash

1. Open the window at top and bottom. Paint all of inner sash and half of outer sash.

2. Reverse positions and paint the rest of the outer sash. Paint the jamb last.

## PAINTING DOUBLE-HUNG WINDOWS

**M**ost **modern** double-hung windows have removable sashes. If you prefer, you can remove each sash, set it up on sawhorses, and paint it "on the flat." To paint a double-hung window in place, the best strategy is to overlap the windows, paint about half of each, and then reverse the overlap, as shown in the drawings.

# Painting Trim

**1** **PROTECT THE FLOOR.** Lay down a drop cloth and mask the floor perimeter. Use medium-tack painter's tape on wood floors but regular masking tape on carpeting. If you are not painting the ceiling or walls, mask these surfaces with low-tack painter's tape or pregummed masking paper.

**2** **SAND TRIM & SET NAILS.** Scuff-sand all trim using 120-grit abrasive to remove the shininess of semigloss or gloss finishes (paint or varnish). To improve the bond on glossy or detailed surfaces, brush on deglosser, following the manufacturer's instructions. Use a nail set and hammer to drive nail heads about ⅛ in. below the surface.

**3** **APPLY THE PRIMER COAT.** Brush primer on all stained, varnished, and unfinished wood surfaces. Previously painted surfaces do not need to be primed. Work from the top down; do the crown molding first, then the chair rail, and finally the baseboard.

**4** **CAULK & PAINT.** Apply a thin (⅛-in.) bead of caulk to seal cracks at trim joints and between trim and wall or ceiling surfaces. Immediately smooth the caulk with a wetted finger. Use a putty knife to press nonshrinking spackle or wood putty into nail holes and other depressions or damaged areas and sand dried repair spots lightly. Brush on two coats of paint, following the directions on the can about recoating time.

**1**

**2**

**3**

**4**

# Painting a Frame & Panel Door

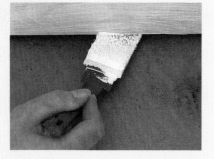

**5** **PREPARE THE DOOR.** If a doorknob and its cover plate are easy to remove, take them off the door by unscrewing the installation screws. Slide heavy paper or a canvas drop cloth under the door. Wedge the door partway open by inserting folded paper or wood shims under the door's bottom edge. Then sand and degloss the door as described for trim.

**6** **APPLY THE PRIMER COAT.** Begin by painting the interior panels. Coat the molded perimeter of each panel first, then paint the flat central area. After painting the panels, coat the stiles, rails, and door edges. Always work from the inside out.

**7** **WIPE PAINT OFF HINGES.** Taking off a door and removing hinges, or even masking them, is not necessary if you immediately wipe paint off the hinges with a damp cloth wrapped over the blade of a putty knife or 5-in-1 tool. Reposition the cloth over the blade each time you wipe.

**8** **APPLY TOP COATS.** When the primer coat has dried completely, it's time to top coat. Two coats will give you a pro appearance. Use a 2-in. paintbrush, and paint from the inside out, starting with the panels. When the last coat has dried, reinstall the doorknob. Nice work!

**5 6**

**7 8**

# Painting a Window

**9**  **REMOVE HARDWARE & SAND.** Remove sash lock hardware and store hardware and screws in a plastic sandwich bag. Also remove and store any window treatment hardware from window jambs. Sand and degloss stained or varnished wood as described for trim.

**10**  **PAINT THE SASH.** By switching the positions of inner and outer sashes, you can paint one half of the outer sash, then the other. Always begin with the innermost mullions and work your way out towards the outer sash frame. Bend the bristles to get paint into corners, and avoid overloading the brush with paint.

**11**  **PAINT THE FRAME & CASING.** With both sashes lowered, coat the head jamb and window trim. Avoid getting any primer or paint on metal or plastic channels. Lower the sash to paint the upper half of the channels and, when the channels are dry, raise the sash to paint the lower half.

**12**  **CLEAN THE GLASS.** Use a fresh blade in your scraper and hold the tool tilted up about 30 degrees from the glass. Doing this minimizes the chance of scratching the glass. To prevent scraping all the paint off the glass and loosing the water seal it provides, hold a 5-in. taping knife or similar tool on the glass and against the frame while you scrape (see also COOL TOOL, p. 36).

**9** **10**

**11** **12**

Pink glows when accompanied by gold and purple paint. The rule here is that a change in surface allows for a change in color, except at the modest baseboard, which accepts the wall color.

*Above right:* He may have out-grown light blue, but a kid still needs some color. Royal blue trim brightens up a white sleeping/ music niche and adds flair to a tall baseboard.

## Be subtle or dramatic. Paint can be used to make trim

blend into the background or to amplify its impact. Possibilities range from painting trim the identical color of the walls to a color that is in contrast to wall colors. Most paint manufacturers have color schemes that take the guesswork out of what colors go well together. The palettes typically include recommendations for walls, trim, and one or more accent colors. You'll also find online tools that allow you to "paint" a particular type of room with wall, ceiling, trim and accent colors.

Paint chips are no match for a color painted in real life because lighting and existing materials have a huge impact. You might not pair green window trim with a red door on paper, but it looks great in this kitchen because colors are muted versions of their primary cousins and because they contrast or complement colors in the existing tile floor.

Colors of the ocean inspire a palette for a seaside bathroom. The chartreuse trim adds a glow to cool-colored blue tile and faux-painted panels.

# Cabinet Makeover

You don't have to spend a fortune to get a **NEW KITCHEN**

REPLACING OLD KITCHEN CABINETS with new cabinetry is a major remodeling project that can cost thousands of dollars. For a kitchen makeover that's just as dramatic but faster and far more affordable, paint is the way to go. Sure, you'll have to shut down the kitchen for several days, but for the price of a little paint, a few other supplies, and a take-out dinner or two, you'll be able to give your kitchen an entirely new identity. The off-white paint job featured in this project brightens up this kitchen, and the bronze metallic glaze applied along the edges of the door panels adds a custom touch. New knobs and drawer handles complete the transformation.

| TAKE IT APART | PREP SURFACES | FRESH COATS | NEW HARDWARE, TOO |

# Tools & Gear

*You can complete this project without a power sander or cordless drill/driver, but you'll find that these two portable power tools make the job go faster and easier.*

**CORDLESS DRILL/DRIVER.** Along with your drill, you'll need an accessory kit that includes drill bits and screw-driving bits for removal and reinstallation of cabinet doors and hardware.

**BOX FAN.** To keep dust from getting everywhere in your house, put a box fan in a kitchen window when you're sanding your cabinets. Make sure it's positioned to pull air outside.

**RANDOM-ORBIT SANDER.** While a power sander is not an absolute necessity, work will go faster and you'll probably do a better job. When sanding doors, drawer fronts, and cabinet face frames, you'll appreciate the maneuverability of a small, palm-size sander like the one shown below.

**WORK LIGHT.** A portable work light reveals imperfections that need to be repaired and helps you avoid missed spots.

**SAWHORSES & 2X4S.** You'll need to set up a work area where cabinet doors and drawers can be painted. Put down a drop cloth first, then place some 2x4s or a piece of plywood across a pair of sawhorses to support doors and drawers.

**DROP CLOTH.** You'll need at least one of these to cover the kitchen floor. You might need another for the floor where you'll be painting cabinet doors and drawer fronts.

**BRUSHES.** A 3-in. brush is good for painting cabinet interiors. For doors and drawer fronts, use a 2-in. angled sash brush. You can use the same sash brush to apply the varnish top coats.

**DUST MASKS.** Make sure that you and your sanding crew wear dust masks when sanding down cabinets.

# What to Buy

**1 | SANDPAPER.** To scuff-sand an entire kitchen's worth of cabinets, you'll need about 8 sheets of 120-grit sandpaper. Aluminum oxide sandpaper will work better than garnet.

**2 | PAINTER'S TAPE.** It's always good to have this tape on hand to mask off surfaces that shouldn't get paint on them.

**3 | PAINTER'S PLASTIC.** Used in conjunction with painter's tape, this inexpensive plastic captures drips and spills so they don't do any damage.

**4 | PRIMER.** Primers are made for different applications. The primer you want here is one formulated to coat stained or varnished wood.

**5 | PAINT.** If you're planning to accent your painted cabinets with a glaze, as we do here, go with an acrylic-latex paint in eggshell sheen. If you just want a plain painted finish, semi-gloss will give you some additional durability and eliminate the need for a varnish top coat.

**6 | PAINT CONDITIONER.** This additive makes acrylic paints easier to apply and helps to eliminate brushmarks. Make sure your conditioner is formulated for use with water-based paints.

**7 | GLAZE.** The bronze-tinted glaze used to accent cabinet doors is available where paints are sold.

**8 | VARNISH.** This clear top coat protects the glaze and paint, giving your cabinets improved durability and making them easier to wipe clean. Buy a satin or semigloss water-based varnish.

## COOL TOOL

**A**lthough **brushes alone** will get you through this job, painting will go faster if you use a foam roller to coat the flat areas of doors and drawer fronts. Available where regular rollers and roller covers are sold, these inexpensive rollers do a good job of getting paint evenly onto cabinet surfaces. They are available in 4-in. and 7-in. lengths.

### LINGO

**Scuff-sanding is a finishing term that means scuffing up a finish so that the next coat you apply will adhere well.**

# Preparing for Paint

## ✻ DO IT FAST

**If you need to drill** new holes for door handles, a simple drilling guide like the one shown below will help you get the job done quickly and accurately. A predrilled hole in the guide directs your drill bit, and the edge guides align the guide against the corner of the door. You can make a similar drill guide for drawer fronts.

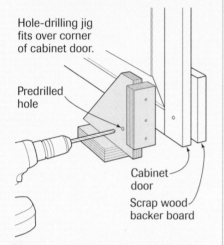

Hole-drilling jig fits over corner of cabinet door.

Predrilled hole

Cabinet door

Scrap wood backer board

## ✻ COOL TOOL

**Molded areas** on doors and drawer fronts are much easier to sand using a sanding sponge. These sanders, available in a variety of grits and shapes, conform to the curved surfaces, won't tear like sandpaper, and can be rinsed out and reused many times.

**1** **EMPTY & DISASSEMBLE CABINETS.** It's amazing what you discover when you empty out your cabinets. Once you've set up temporary storage for cabinet contents, remove cabinet doors, drawers, and shelves that will be painted. Remove hinges, pulls, and handles. Store this hardware (and the installation screws that go with it) in sandwich bags. Set up the painting area for doors and drawers, and set up an exhaust fan in a kitchen window.

**2** **DO SOME BORING WORK.** If new door and drawer hardware will require holes in different locations, fill existing holes with a nonshrinking wood filler. Sand the wood filler flush after it dries and drill new holes using a homemade drilling jig as shown in the photo. (See also DO IT FAST, at left.)

**3** **SCUFF-SAND, VACUUM & CLEAN.** Paint won't bond well to stained and varnished wood unless you scuff-sand the old finish first. Use 120-grit sandpaper. To save time, power-sand flat areas with a random-orbit or palm sander. Equip your sander with a dust bag. Better yet: Attach a shop vacuum to the sander's dust port. After sanding, vacuum the entire room. Wipe surfaces to be painted with a tack cloth and then with a clean, lint-free cloth dampened with mineral spirits.

**4** **MASK & PROTECT OTHER SURFACES.** Run masking tape along cabinet/wall junctures. Cover countertops and appliances with cardboard or newspaper. Protect floors with canvas drop cloths.

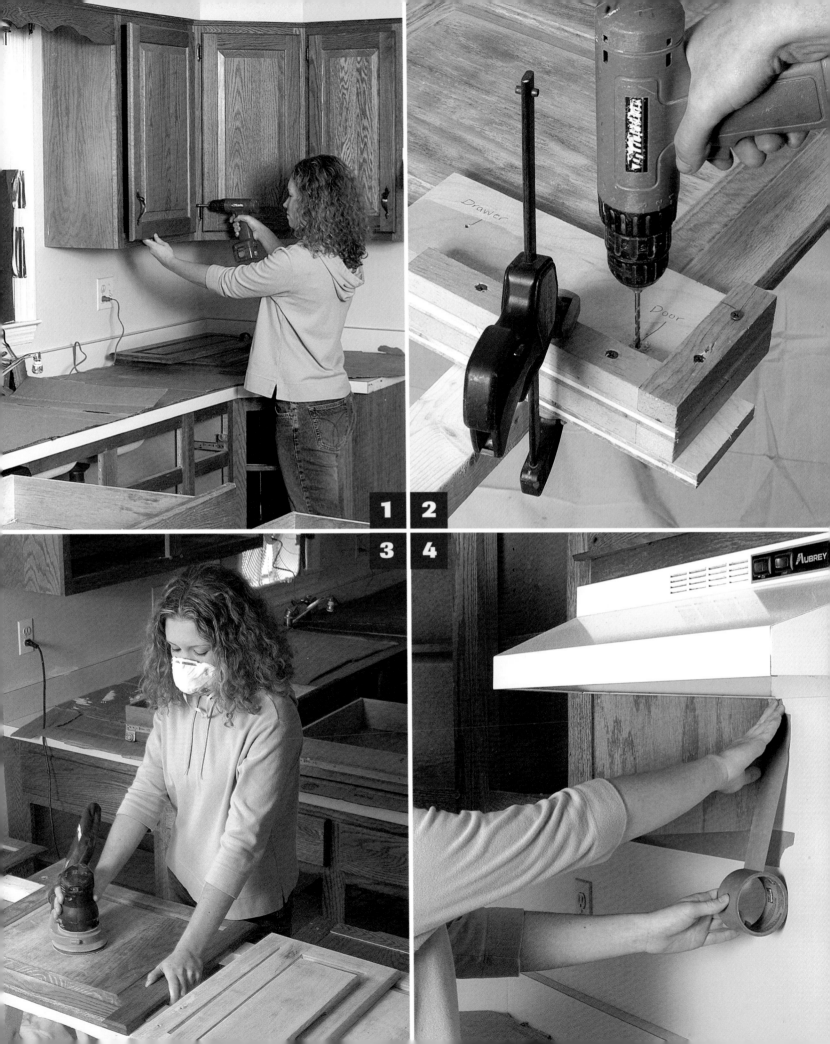

## ⊙ DO IT RIGHT

**While the drawers** are out, take a few minutes with your screwdriver to tighten loose screws that secure the drawer slides to the drawers and cabinet.

## + WHAT CAN GO WRONG

**Drips and runs** can spoil a finish. To minimize them, brush out from inside corners, not toward them. Check just-painted surfaces every couple minutes to brush out any drips before the paint skins over.

# Now the Fun Part

**5** **APPLY PRIMER.** The toughest painting comes first, because you need to work from the inside out. Prime-coat the interiors of cabinets and drawers, then move on to surfaces that show. Use a brush to cut in along corners, then finish up using a wider brush or a foam roller to get primer on flat surfaces.

**6** **APPLY PAINT.** Repeat the previous painting sequence, but with paint instead of primer. Work quickly on inside areas and more carefully where your work will show. If your brush drags or leaves brush marks, add latex paint conditioner to the paint, following the manufacturer's directions. Apply a second coat if necessary, after lightly sanding out any visible drips and brush marks. Remove all dust with a vacuum and a tack cloth before recoating.

**7** **GLAZE THE PANEL EDGES.** Mix 3 parts glazing medium with one part paint for each of your glaze colors and pour some onto paper dinner plates. Brush the glaze into the molded perimeter of each door panel; then wipe most of it off with a damp sponge. You can keep applying and wiping down until you get the look you like.

**8** **SEAL YOUR WORK.** There's no need to clear-coat your cabinets if you've applied a semigloss paint, but any glaze treatment should be protected with some fast-drying clear acrylic finish. Apply it with a good brush, making sure to brush carefully along corners and edges to avoid drips. For maximum protection, apply several coats, following the manufacturer's directions for recoating.

**9** **INSTALL HARDWARE, DOORS & DRAWERS.** Install hinges on doors, reinstall doors and drawers, and install new handles or pulls. Wait for the paint to dry completely before lining and loading shelves that have been painted.

**5**

**6**

**7**

**9**

**8**

It's easy to change your cabinet hardware to complete your cabinet makeover with the wide variety of pulls, handles, and knobs available today. Adding knobs or pulls to doors and drawers that previously used finger pulls will keep them looking nice longer. Replace old hinges with self-closing ones, adding self-stick rubber bumpers to the backs of the doors so they close more quietly.

Solid doors conceal cabinet clutter so they are suitable for most cabinet doors. But consider swapping out some solid doors for glass ones to make a display cabinet for china and glassware or for canisters or jars of dry food. Interior lighting and a bold interior paint color make the contents of these cabinets really stand out.

**If you're planning** a paint-based cabinet makeover, be sure to factor in all the details of your kitchen decor. Are there natural wood tones to work with? What about new or existing light fixtures? How about making new cabinet hardware part of your makeover? Ask and answer questions like these and you're sure to make the most of your makeover.

This inspired contemporary kitchen design blends two cabinet finishes—a low luster soft green paint and varnished wood—with stone countertops, stainless-steel shelf edging and hardware, and a frosted-glass backsplash. Mixing two finishes also works if you've got a large island you want to set apart.

# Old-World Wall

Who would guess you created that **RUSTIC PLASTER** appearance with pieces of crumpled plastic?

THE FORMULA IS SIMPLE, and the results are beautiful. The old-world wall finish earns its name for the unique texture it creates. Applying this finish is a great way to transform a plain painted wall into a surface that looks like rough plaster. You've got to touch the wall to realize that the depth and texture are just an illusion. Working this magic takes some practice, which is best done on watercolor paper or on a wall that you plan to repaint anyway. You'll also discover that it's easier and more fun to create an old-world wall with a partner instead of on your own. One person can apply the glaze, while the other follows behind, creating the texture.

BASE-COATING  MIXING GLAZE  BRUSH IT ON  OLD-WORLD TEXTURE

# Tools & Gear

*In addition to the tools and supplies specifically required for the old-world wall finish, see the project beginning on p. 22 for details on tools, supplies, and guidelines for prepping and painting walls.*

**CANVAS DROP CLOTH.** Have one or more of these to spread on the floor and enough for a double layer over carpeting because spilled paint may bleed through even the best canvas. Plastic is way too slippery to use underfoot.

**BRUSHES.** To create an old-world wall, you'll need two brushes: Use a 3-in. or 4-in. brush for applying the glaze and a 2-in. or 3-in. brush for cutting and texturing around trim and at inside corners. You can paint with either natural- or synthetic-bristle brushes when working with alkyd paint, but for latex paint, use only a synthetic (usually a polyester-nylon blend), such as the 4-in. brush in the photo.

**ROLLER & TRAY.** To apply the base coat on walls and, if applicable, to paint ceilings, you'll need a 9-in. roller.

**PAINTER'S POLE.** Poles extend your reach and thereby eliminate lots of bending and ladder work. Adjustable ones adapt to more situations, but an ordinary broomstick works well for standard 8-ft. or 10-ft.-high walls and ceilings.

## ▶ DO IT RIGHT

**Don't commit to a color scheme** or a decorative technique till you take a test drive on paper. Try out your glaze and base coat combinations and your texturing tactics on 11x17 sheets of artist's watercolor paper, available at art supply stores. Remember to write down the mixing proportions of glaze and tinting paint so you can duplicate this mix when it's time to paint for real.

## ▪ LINGO

**To extend the open time of a water-based glaze, you can add retarder, which will slow drying. More open time is especially helpful when you're working alone, because you'll need the glaze to remain workable for a longer period of time.**

## WHAT CAN GO WRONG

**It can be difficult** to maintain consistent texture and tone, and it is very difficult to "repair" a dry faux finish. For consistency when working with another person, let one apply the glaze and the other work it. Keep looking back. If you see that an area is too light (and the glaze is still wet), dab on some extra glaze and rework the texture with crumpled plastic. If an area is too dark, go back over it with plastic; this should remove a little more glaze. Worst-case scenario: Reapply a base coat on the unacceptable wall, and try again.

# What to Buy

*You can buy everything you need for this project at the paint store or in the paint and finishes section at your local home center. The quantities listed here should be adequate for a small (12x14) room like the one shown on the following pages.*

**1│ PAINT.**  As with many faux finishes, this technique requires a base coat (often two coats) with moderate sheen, either eggshell or semigloss. Pick up a gallon of 100% acrylic (or alkyd) interior paint. You'll need another gallon (usually a darker tone or color) to mix with the glaze.

**2│ GLAZING LIQUID.**  Glazing liquid has a paint-like consistency, but it's designed to be tinted, typically by mixing it with paint. The resulting glaze is applied over a base coat, and then manipulated to create different decorative effects. Get a gallon of water-based or alkyd glaze, based on the type of paint you are using.

**3│ PAINT THINNER.**  If you're using alkyd paint and glaze (as we did on this project), buy a gallon of paint thinner for cleaning brushes and thinning the glaze. No thinner is necessary if you're using water-based paint.

**4│ RETARDER.**  If you use a water-based glaze, you'll need to add retarder (see LINGO, on the facing page) to prevent the coating from drying out too quickly on a large project like this.

## OTHER SUPPLIES

**PAINTER'S TAPE.**  Pick up a roll or two of this special tape to cover trim and other surfaces that you don't want covered with wall paint and glaze.

**ROLLER COVERS.**  Pick up a couple medium nap (³/₈ in. or ¹/₂ in.) 9-in. roller covers for base-coating walls and an extra one if you are painting the ceiling.

**RAGS.**  Keep handy a clean rag dampened with solvent (water or mineral spirits) to wipe up drips and spatters. If the rag gets too full of paint, replace it with a fresh one. Paint stores usually sell boxes or bags of absorbent rags.

**MIXING BUCKETS.**  Inexpensive plastic buckets with volume measurements printed on them make it easy to get the proportions right when mixing glaze.

**PLASTIC GARBAGE BAGS.**  You'll need a few of these to hold used masking tape and discarded wads of plastic that have been used to texture the glaze.

**PAINTER'S PLASTIC.**  This thin, clear sheeting comes on a roll or folded. It's useful for protecting chandeliers and furniture during painting projects. But to create an old-world wall, you'll be crumpling up the plastic and using it to work the glaze.

⊙ **DO IT RIGHT**

**It's easy to misplace** the tiny cover plate screws. As you remove outlet covers, store them in a plastic bag or other container.

**⊛ WHAT'S DIFFERENT?**

**Regular high-tack masking tape** is great for masking carpeting or rough surfaces but may adhere so strongly to painted trim or walls that it can damage the surface when it is removed. Painter's tape, available in several degrees of tackiness, protects

surfaces without damaging them. Use medium-tack tape on painted or varnished surfaces that have cured more than 30 days and low-tack tape on delicate surfaces and freshly painted ones.

# Ready, Set, Go!

**1** **PROTECT ELECTRICAL OUTLETS.** Remove cover plates on electrical outlets and cover the devices with painter's tape. Cover any wall-mounted light fixtures with plastic and mask their trim, too

**2** **MASK & PROTECT.** Use 2-in.-wide painter's tape to mask the trim in all areas to be painted and glazed. To make sure the tape is well adhered, burnish the edge of the tape with a fingernail or the handle of a screwdriver. If there's no cornice trim, mask off the ceiling so that you won't get any glaze on it. When you're done taping, place a drop cloth on the floor along the wall.

**3** **APPLY THE BASE COAT.** Paint your walls with an eggshell or semi-gloss paint that is compatible with your glaze. Glazing does not change normal painting standards: If two coats would normally be required for full and uniform coverage on an unglazed wall, then two coats are required for a base coat.

**4** **MIX THE GLAZE.** For this project, we mixed equal parts glazing liquid, paint, and paint thinner. You should duplicate the proportions that you tried earlier on your test panel. Blend all three glaze ingredients together in a clean plastic paint bucket. For good workability, glaze should have a more liquid consistency than paint.

**1**

**2**

**3**

**4**

**Make sure that the room** has good ventilation so that paint fumes won't become concentrated. This is especially important when using alkyd paint and glaze.

**⊙ DO IT RIGHT**

**If you need a coffee or lunch break,** plan to stop at the edge of a window or door or complete a full wall. Don't stop in the middle of the wall. To stop at an inside corner, mask off the next wall right at the corner.

# Putting It on the Walls

**5** **APPLY THE GLAZE.** Using use a 3-in. or 4-in. brush, make a series of closely spaced diagonal applications. Dip your brush in glaze and tap it lightly on the side of the can. Don't wipe it. Apply a thick coat of glaze, and don't worry about spreading it out to cover the base coat completely. The glaze will be spread out evenly when you do the texturing.

**6** **TEXTURE THE GLAZE WITH CRUMPLED PLASTIC.** Here's where the fun begins. The wad of plastic you use should be sized so you can hold it in one hand. The texturing action you want involves both dabbing and spreading, so that bare areas between glaze applications can get filled in. Aim for a mottled surface texture that has depth, showing both the base coat and the glaze. When a handful of plastic gets too wet to work with, replace it with a fresh wad.

**7** **TEXTURE THE HARD-TO-REACH AREAS.** You won't be able to reach into corners with the crumpled plastic. Instead, do the texturing with a dry brush. A dab-and-twist action works well. Have a rag handy to wipe excess glaze from the brush if  it gets too wet. In narrow areas above doorways, you can texture with a smaller piece of plastic.

**8** **ADMIRE YOUR WORK!** Nice job. There's a lot more character here than you get with plain painted walls. Remove the masking tape as you complete each wall. Use a rag moistened with water (for latex glaze) or paint thinner (for alkyd glaze) to wipe up any drips or splatters off trim and other surfaces.

**5** **6**

**7** **8**

An old-world wall can be as light and delicate as the top sample or as rich and velvety as the bottom sample. It all depends on the color combination you choose.

**It's fun to make** a new wall look old. The way you manipulate the glaze—with plastic or rags, and with subtle or bold ragging technique—will determine the final texture you create. As for color combinations, stick with colors that aren't too vibrant if you want a traditional look. You'll see from these pages that a wall looks deeper and richer when the base coat and glaze are similar in value, but don't be afraid to experiment with different tones and colors. "Replastering" is easy with paint.

Using glazes with different drying times can result in a crackle finish that adds age and character. Crackle finish kits are available where paints are sold.

Three shades of brown were used to age this stairway wall. Medium brown and dark umber glazes (the two darker tones) were applied and textured over a lighter base coat.

This red-toned wall treatment compliments the color of a mahogany cabinet.

This rich, camel-colored wall is the perfect complement to ornate warm-white painted moldings.

# Strié & Chambray

Dragging a glaze using **DRY-BRUSH TECHNIQUES** opens a world of painting possibilities

L OOKING FOR AN EASY WAY to add interest to a painted room? Look no farther than the decorative painting technique called strié or dragging. Using this technique, a colored glaze is applied over a base coat of eggshell or semigloss paint. Then the wet glaze is immediately worked with a dry brush to create a delicate and detailed vertical pattern. A half-height wall, such as the area below a chair rail, is a particularly good candidate for dragging, because you can easily drag your brush from top to bottom without getting on a ladder.

| PREP THE WALL | ROLL ON THE GLAZE | TEXTURE TECHNIQUE | YOU'RE DONE! |

### ▰ **LINGO**

**Strié, also known as dragging or striating, is a decorative technique that involves dragging a dry brush vertically over a freshly applied glaze to expose some of the base coat color below. Chambray is similar but you follow up with a horizontal pass to produce a woven texture (see the bottom photos on p. 72).**

# Tools & Gear

**STEPLADDER.** While not required for this wainscot application, you'll need this if your work takes you up to the ceiling.

**CANVAS DROP CLOTH.** Protect your floors with a canvas drop cloth. Plastic is too slippery underfoot. If your floor is carpeted, double or triple the protection to prevent spills from leaking through the canvas.

**PAINT ROLLER & TRAY.** Plastic trays seem easier to clean and don't rust. A 4-in. roller worked fine for this wainscoting project, but for a full-height wall, use a standard 9-in. roller.

### ▶ **DO IT RIGHT**

**New roller covers,** even quality ones, shed fuzz, which ends up on your wall in the wet paint. To minimize the problem press tape onto the roller and then peel off loose material.

**PAINTBRUSHES.** For texturing the glaze, you need a 3-in. or wider brush with relatively stiff, coarse bristles. Specialty brushes like the one above are also available where paint supplies are sold.

## WHAT'S DIFFERENT?

**O**il-based paints and glazes have been preferred by most professional decorative painters chiefly because of the longer "open" time— a period that the glaze stays wet enough to work with a sponge, rag, or other texturing tools. But if you don't like to work with alkyd finishes, don't worry. You can mix an extender (paint conditioner) into water-based glaze to increase its open time.

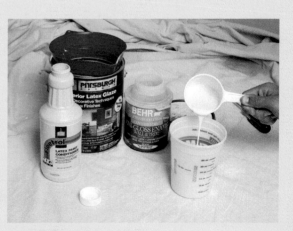

# What to Buy

**1| PAINTER'S TAPE.** Painter's tape is designed to seal well at the edges so paint won't bleed underneath, but it will not pull off any paint or damage surfaces when it is removed. Use medium-tack tape on painted trim that has cured for at least 30 days and low-tack tape on freshly painted trim.

**2| GLAZING LIQUID.** Glazing liquid has a paint-like consistency and is available in acrylic (water-based) and alkyd (oil-based) versions. When mixed with paint, the resulting glaze produces a somewhat translucent finish that allows the color of the base coat to show through. The higher the glaze-to-paint ratio is, the more translucent the finish.

**3| PAINT.** You need two colors: typically a light color base coat in eggshell sheen and a darker color you'll use to tint the glazing liquid.

**4| PAINT THINNER.** You'll need this for thinning glaze, dampening rags to remove drips, and cleaning brushes only if you're using an alkyd glaze.

**5| PAINT-MIXING BUCKET.** Washable plastic buckets with volume measurements make it easy to measure the right proportions of paint and glaze.

## COOL TOOL

**K**eep your paint and roller fresh in a covered paint tray while you brush out each rolled section, or even during a coffee or lunch break. You'll find these plastic trays at your paint store.

**For consistent results,** it's important to keep your texturing brush dry. Wipe the glaze off the bristles with a damp rag as you complete each pass. If you're texturing a large area it may even be necessary to clean the brush.

# Four Simple Steps

**1** **PREPARE THE WALL.** Remove any cover plates and mask the fixture. Complete any needed trim or wall repairs, prime them, and paint the trim (if planned). Mask trim to protect it during wall painting. Burnish the tape with a fingernail to make sure the tape is well adhered at the edge. Roll on a base coat of eggshell or semigloss latex paint.

**2** **MIX & APPLY GLAZE.** Pour 1-part paint and 1-part glazing liquid into a paint bucket and mix well. Use a medium-nap roller (⅜ in. to ½-in.) to apply the glaze over a 3-ft.-wide area from the top to the bottom of the wall, which in this case is from the masked chair rail molding to masked base molding. No need to cut in with a brush.

**3** **TEXTURE THE PAINT.** Immediately fill in the unpainted areas at the very top and very bottom with the strie or dragging brush. Then drag the brush down the wall from top to bottom in a single pass, maintaining even pressure. Overlap the previously brushed area very slightly to avoid creating a noticeable transition from one pass to the next. Roll and brush your way along the wall the same way.

**4** **REMOVE MASKING TAPE.** As you complete each wall, remove the masking tape. Always pull at a low angle and slowly to avoid pulling any paint off the trim with the tape. If necessary, touch up any areas where paint may have bled under the tape.

**1**

**2**

**3**

**4**

**Wide blue stripes made with the strié technique add a soft, fabric look to the wall in a child's room.**

**This vertical strié pattern above the wainscoting and mantel looks very much like rough, natural silk.**

**In this close-up you can clearly see the detail of t technique shown in the photo on the facing pag**

**Walls painted with the chambray technique (that's strié done with two passes at right angles) really do look like woven fabric.**

# Weave walls anywhere. The strié wainscoting shown in

the step-by-step pages represents only one of almost limitless possibilities for this technique. While well suited to walls, strié is also effective on doors, tabletops, and other surfaces. Experiment with different "tools," such as a flagging brush, a cellulose sponge, or a rag. Each tool produces a unique pattern. For a more dramatic effect, try using contrasting colors for your base coat and glaze. You can even combine techniques such as strié and the stripes shown on p. 102. As with most decorative painting, practice on paper before committing your design to your wall.

A cheery alcove is finished with an apple-green glaze dragged over a white base coat. This airy finish makes a nice backdrop for the dark dresser.

# An Artist's Touch

Make any stencil unique with easy **SHADING, TONING & SPLATTER** painting techniques

S TENCILING IS A GREAT WAY to embellish a door, wall, floor, or any flat surface by combining just a little paint with a lot of imagination. Take a look around the house, or even in a single room, and imagine how a bare wall could get a wake-up call with some creative stenciling. You can buy ready-made stencils in many shapes and styles. Or you can make your own stencils from favorite paintings, photos, or other images (see p. 83). In the stenciling project shown here, you'll see how to create a hand-painted appearance using a combination of colored glazes, paint spatters, and brushed-on details.

**TAPE IT UP**          **COLOR IT IN**          **ADD SOME DETAIL**          **CLEAR-COAT**

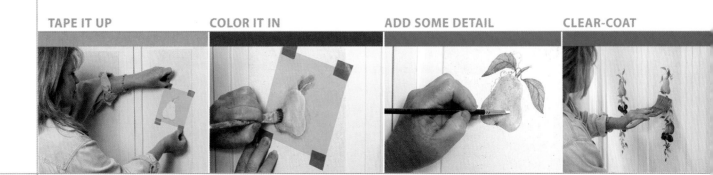

# Tools & Gear

**GLOVES.** You can skip these if you don't mind getting some paint on your hands. Otherwise, disposable vinyl gloves are the way to go.

**STENCILING BRUSHES.** These brushes come in different sizes. If your paint center doesn't have them, try an art supply store. For the fruit-size stenciling done here, $\frac{3}{4}$-in.- or 1-in.-wide brushes work best. You'll need a separate brush for each color.

**OLD TOOTHBRUSH.** Always handy to have around, this brush will serve as your spatter-painting tool.

**ARTIST'S BRUSH.** Get a fine-pointed round brush you can use for painting veins and small stems.

## ⊛ WHAT'S DIFFERENT?

**If your stencil project** involves just one or two standard colors, consider buying **stencil paint** rather than mixing your own colored glazes. Stencil paint comes ready to stir up and apply. If you're painting fruit or flowers, it's better to buy acrylic paint and glazing medium so you can make your own glazes. This enables you to fine-tune the intensity of the color you apply.

## DO IT NOW

**P**ractice your brush technique on primed wood, a drywall scrap, or poster board. You'll learn how much paint to put on the brush and, even then, how much to dab off on your paper towel. You'll learn that a small, swirling motion applies paint evenly without getting it under the stencil. In the process you can evaluate color choices. You can even cut out your creation to see what it looks like in place.

# What to Buy

*The first items on this list might give the impression you're plan-ning to barbecue some ribs, but they'll help you work quickly and with as little mess as possible.*

**1| DISPOSABLE DINNER PLATES.** Plastic or plastic-coated paper plates give you the shallow palette you need for mix-ing paints and glaze.

**2| PAPER TOWELS.** It's important to limit the amount of paint on your brush when stenciling. After dabbing your brush into paint or glaze, you need to blot off some of the color on paper towels.

**3| PAINT & GLAZE.** Small bottles or tubes of acrylic paint (sometimes called artist's colors) will give you adequate quantities for any small stenciling project. The colors used in this project include white, yellow, red, brown and several shades of green. You'll also need a water-based glaze.

**4| ACRYLIC VARNISH.** To make the finished stencil wash-able and durable, you'll need several top coats of clear, water-based varnish. Buy satin or semigloss varnish rather than

gloss. Where extra protec-tion is required, look for a floor varnish or sealer.

**5| STENCILS.** Precut stencils are available in hundreds of designs. If fruit, flowers, and vines aren't right for what you have in mind, there are geometric designs, ornate letters, and architectural elements to consider—just to name a few options. Don't rule out the possibility of making your own stencils, too (see p. 83). No matter where you get your sten-cils, the application and paint techniques shown here will work well for you.

**6| PAINTER'S TAPE.** Use this tape to adhere the stencil to the wall, cabinet door, or other surface. You can also use it to tape up plastic or newspaper to protect adjacent areas while you're painting.

## ∷ LINGO

Registration marks enable you to remove and reposition a stencil and get it in exactly the right position every time. Store-bought stencils come with precut notches or holes where you can make registration marks. If you make your own stencils, use a sharp pair of scissors to cut two V-shaped notches in the stencil.

## ✛ WHAT CAN GO WRONG

It's easy to apply too much glaze and cover the stencil surface too evenly. To get a more natural look and more variety in repeated stencils, apply different color glazes in small amounts and don't spend too much time blending colors together inside the stencil.

# Painting Your First Stencil

**1** **PREPARE STENCIL & GLAZE.** Position the first stencil plate—a pear, in this case. Adhere the top edge with painter's tape and lightly pencil the two registration marks at the perimeter. For more realism, several colors are used for the pear. For each color, mix one part acrylic paint with two parts glaze and pour the resulting colored glazes onto separate plastic dinner plates.

**2** **APPLY THE FIRST COLOR.** Dip the tip of your brush into the glaze and blot it on a paper towel to remove excess. Keeping the brush perpendicular to the surface, apply paint with short circular motions or, for a more textured effect, a dabbing motion. Both techniques prevent paint from getting under the stencil.

**3** **ADD & BLEND COLORS.** Dab your brush dry with some paper towels, then apply glaze in different colors, using the same perpendicular brush technique as in step 2. With a dabbing and twisting motion, you can blend your colors inside the stencil. Making one side of the fruit darker adds depth and realism. Remember not to tilt the brush as you're blending.

**4** **SPATTER-PAINT.** A toothbrush is just the tool you need to mimic the speckles and little imperfections on a typical pear. After your glaze has had a chance to dry, dip your toothbrush into some brown-toned glaze and draw your thumb across the bristles to direct your spatter at a piece of newspaper. When you get a pleasing density of spatters, turn to the stencil. When you finish, remove the stencil.

# Adding Details

**5** **STENCIL THE LEAVES.** Adhere the second stencil plate (for the leaves), aligning notches in its perimeter with the registration marks you penciled in Step 1. Prepare the leaf glaze colors and paint the second stencil as you did in earlier steps. Remove and clean your stencils.

**6** **PAINT THE VEINS.** Mix up some darker green glaze to add veining detail to each leaf. Use a fine-tipped artist's brush and start with the largest central vein that bisects the leaf from step to tip. Next, add small veins that extend from the central vein to the leaf edge. To taper veins, try this trick: Lift the brush away from the surface and your vein will grow finer.

**7** **ADD FINISHING TOUCHES.** Clean the brush and add a little star of brown at the bottom end of the pear. Use another brush to add some white highlights. If you like, you can even paint in a curl of fiber from the main stem of the pear. These little details are optional but they enable you to make each stencil unique.

**8** **SEAL THE STENCIL.** Allow the paint to dry overnight. Then, using a varnish brush, apply at least three coats of clear acrylic varnish. This nonyellowing finish won't dull your colors. Follow the manufacturer's directions about drying time between coats.

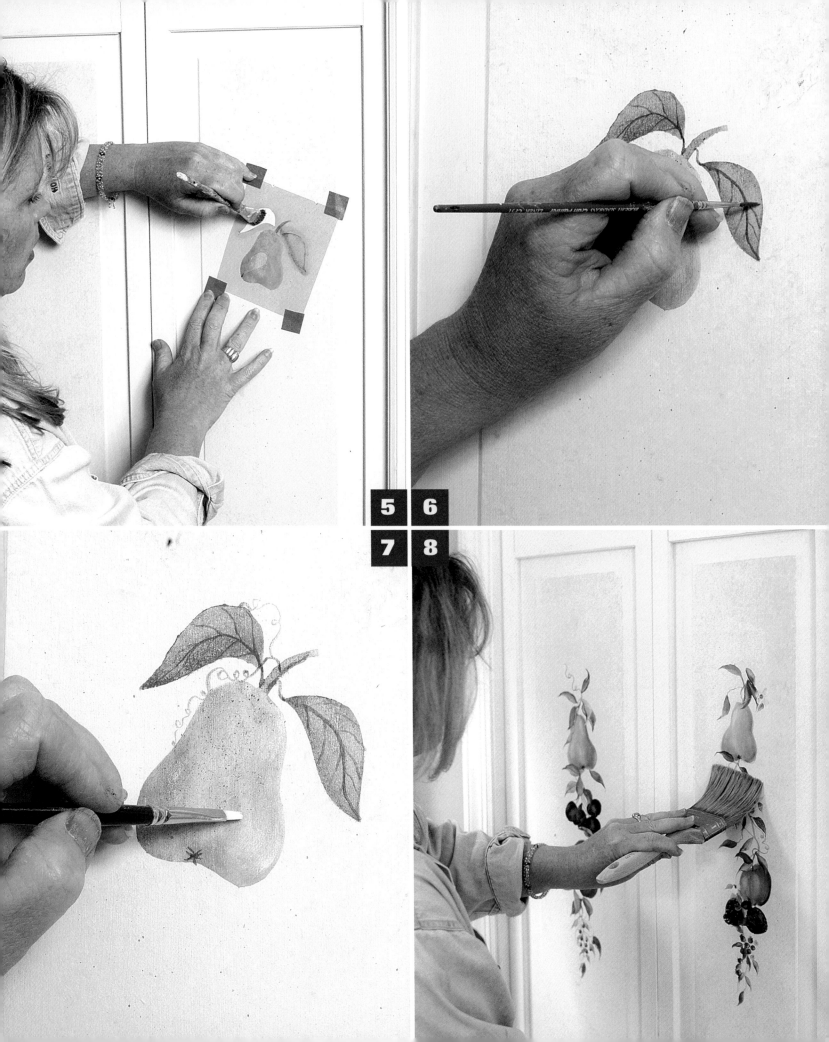

5 6
7 8

A key to success in stenciling a big repeating pattern such as these two is to align registration marks perfectly.

After base-layer paint dries, it's time to try out stencils. Stencils can overlap base colors to make two-toned creatures and plants (above left) or to indicate time passing (above right).

## Stencils can go anywhere. It's certainly true that stencils can wake up a wall or create an eye-catching detail on a cabinet door. They can also be used in many other situations. Furniture, floors, mailboxes, and ceilings can gain a fresh identity from different stencil treatments.

**Using drywall compound** creates a stencil that stands proud of the surrounding surface. Instead of painting inside the stencil border, apply a thin layer of hard-setting drywall joint compound that can be sanded, shaped, and painted after drying.

**You can make your own stencils.** If you find a painting, drawing, or photo with great stencil potential, it's not difficult to use that image to generate a stencil. Use a color copier to create a working print of the design. You can go with the same size, enlarge, or reduce the image. Trace the outline of the image onto some clear film (above left), which is available at office supply stores, then use a mat knife to make the cutout (left). The cutout will serve as your template for tracing the design onto some poster board or other stencil material.

# The Sky's the Limit

It just takes **A LITTLE BIT OF BRUSHWORK** to create a beautiful day indoors

CLOUDS, REAL OR FAUX, INSPIRE DAYDREAMS and help us look far beyond ourselves. That's why it's fun to create your own interior cloudscape. Bedrooms, bathrooms, and home offices all have excellent sky potential. Once you've had some cloud-crafting practice, you'll have the power to create a sunny day on one side of the room, ominous thunderheads on the other side, and any variation in between. Serious weather addicts may want to paint the walls blue, too; this will give you more room for clouds.

APPLY BASE COAT     PAINT WHITE FIRST     THEN DARK FOR DEPTH     FINISHING TOUCHES

❖ COOL TOOL

**A natural sponge** is a great application tool when you're painting clouds. It is especially effective at softening the transition between clouds and sky or for adding shadows in clouds.

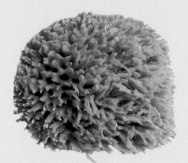

# Tools & Gear

*If the ceiling you're working on is already blue but cloudless, you're ahead of the game. If you need to create a blue sky overhead, the Paint a Room project that begins on p. 22 will be helpful. The tools and gear listed below will get you through the job.*

**3-IN. BRUSH.** This is a good size brush for cutting in where ceilings and walls meet. Get a top-quality synthetic-bristle brush designed for water-based paints.

**ROLLER, TRAY & POLE.** Add a roller cover to these tools and you've got what it takes to apply the base coat and the background sky.

**OLD BRUSHES.** When it's time to create your clouds, a bad brush is going to be better than a good one. That's because you want the spotty, irregular coverage that these brushes create. Get a cheap 2-in. "chip" brush and an old varnish or stain brush that's 1½ in. to 2 in. wide.

**DROP CLOTH.** No room-painting project should get done without a canvas drop cloth or two. Unfold your tarps and shake them out outside before you bring them into the house.

**STEPLADDER.** You'll need one of these to get close to the ceiling to brush on your clouds and add shading to bring them to life.

▶ DO IT RIGHT

**It only takes a few trips** outside to see that sky blue can be a varied hue. Plan on mixing some white and blue together in a separate container to create a lighter sky. You can also darken the sky by adding some black paint to your blue.

## COOL TOOL

**P**our spouts for paint cans allow you to stir paint in a full can, wipe excess paint off your brush, and pour paint—all without getting paint into the lid channel or down the outside of the can! A well-stocked paint store will have these helpful lids along with other aids.

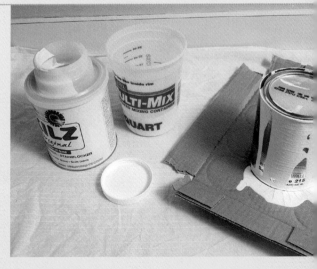

# What to Buy

*Check out the project that begins on p. 22 if you want to repaint the entire room. If you're just interested in creating a partly cloudy day, go with the shopping list described below.*

**1| PAINT.** For the background sky, buy flat acrylic latex paint in a medium blue hue. It's better to err on the side of a darker blue, because you can always lighten the hue by mixing in some white paint. A gallon is usually plenty to give the ceiling of an average-size bedroom a couple of coats. To paint the clouds, buy a quart of the brightest flat white acrylic paint available; it's often called "super white." For the dark colors (grays, purples, and blues) that help define a cloud's shape and give it a three-dimensional appearance, pick up a small bottle each of black, dark blue, and red artist's colors. You can mix a dab or two of the color with a puddle of white paint to get the desired color.

**2| PAINTER'S PLASTIC.** Use this to cover any furniture that you can't get out of the room.

**3| DISPOSABLE DINNER PLATES.** Foam, plastic, or plastic-coated paper plates will all work fine, and you need just a few for mixing your artist's colors with each other and with white for subtle shading work. (You didn't think clouds were entirely white, did you?)

**4| PLASTIC PAINT BUCKETS.** Have a couple of these inexpensive containers on hand so that you can mix up some different shades of blue if the fancy strikes you.

**5| PAPER TOWELS.** A roll of paper towels can be a painter's best friend when spills need blotting up. But for this project, you'll also use the towels to remove paint from the brushes that carry accent colors.

## ▶ DO IT RIGHT

**If your goal** is a super-realistic sky, try these tips:

**1** Make some clouds bright white around their top edges, where the sun hits them. Undersides are good candidates for darker accents.

**2** For high, thin clouds, use a more transparent white finish: Mix water or glazing medium with white paint.

**3** If your clouds are windswept, keep the wind direction consistent.

# Creating a Skyscape

**1** **APPLY THE SKY.** If you don't want your walls blue like the ceiling, the first step will be to cut in around the ceiling using your 3-in. brush. Just a brush-width of blue is all you need to keep the ends of the roller from touching the walls. Then start to roll the blue onto the ceiling, dipping the roller into the paint tray, rolling out the excess paint, and rolling from one end of the room to the other. Make big Ws, then fill them in.

**2** **OUTLINE THE CLOUDS.** Don't work one cloud at a time. Instead, brush a little paint on the ceiling to locate the major clouds and define each one's general shape. You can use your 3-in. brush or one of your older brushes. When you've got the cloud density you want, brush or roll white paint to fill in each cloud's outline.

**3** **DEFINE SHAPES WITH ACCENT COLORS.** Mix some artist's colors in a small puddle of white paint on a disposable plate to create some cloud-shading accent hues. Dark blue-grey or dark purple look good. After dipping an old brush into the accent color, wipe your brush dry on paper towels and then dab it onto the white clouds to create darker,

denser areas and create a more interesting skyscape. You can also go back and add pure white again, if necessary. To create a windswept appearance, blend accents in with a dry brush, using a swirling motion. This can also be done with a natural sponge.

**4** **ADD CLOUDS & FINE-TUNE.** Step back from your work often and view it from different perspectives. Keep improving the weather by adding blue, white, and accent hues here and there. If the walls are blue, you can extend some clouds down onto upper wall surfaces too.

**1**

**2**

**3**

**4**

In a baby's bedroom, a soothing ever-present rainbow trims the wall, topped by an alternate vision of the night sky, with blue stars on white clouds.

**The most convincing clouds** generally start with light-to-medium color sky-blue walls and ceilings. This minimizes and softens the ceiling-wall transition and enables you to bring the clouds down the wall here and there. That said, there is no right or wrong way to paint clouds. We each have a vision of what a cloud looks like, and the clouds we paint should reflect that vision.

A subtle, realistic cloudscape will be enjoyed by the very young and by older members of the family, and therefore may have a longer-lasting appeal.

This cloud is rendered in wood to make a decorative railing. A matching cloud is sponged onto the wall beyond. The soft green walls change to blue by sponging on paint as needed.

Clouds and blue sky become an abstract pattern when spread across cabinets and walls. This takes careful planning and a frequent step back to survey the effect as a whole. Flying geese add reality to the scene.

# Faux Tile Backsplash

Here's a **TILE BACKSPLASH** you can install for the price of paint

P AINTING A FAUX TILE BACKSPLASH may be one example of fake being better than the real thing. How so? Well, to begin, you can get the exact look you want, color coordinated with other design elements in your kitchen. Your tile "installation" can get done in a day, for a fraction of the cost of real tile. And with a coat or two of clear finish, you'll have a surface that's stain-resistant and easy to clean.

| MEASURE & MARK | TAPE GROUT LINES | SPONGE-PAINT | CLEAR PROTECTION |

# Tools & Gear

*Faux tile is a lot easier to "install" than the real thing, mainly because there's no need to cut tiles to size or apply mastic and grout. In addition to some basic painting tools, you'll also need some measuring and layout gear to get your grout lines true.*

**TAPE MEASURE.** A 12-ft. or longer tape will enable you to mark where grout lines fall on your wall.

**LEVEL & STRAIGHTEDGE.** Either a 2-ft. or 4-ft. level will keep your horizontal layout lines on the level. To extend these lines as necessary, use a straightedge.

**WORK LIGHT.** It's not a must-have tool, but a portable light can add some valuable illumination when you're working under wall cabinets.

**CARDBOARD.** Cut this to size to protect the countertop. If you can't find enough cardboard, a roll of kraft paper will do the job.

**PAINT-ROLLING KIT.** Get your paint roller and roller tray ready. You'll need these to apply a base coat for the tile treatment.

## ◆ DO IT NOW

**Not sure about what color** scheme to use for your tile? Designers make up sample boards to give clients a clear picture of what is planned. You can do the same and practice your tile-painting technique at the same time. Paint on heavy poster board, drywall, hardboard, or any smooth paintable material.

## WHAT'S DIFFERENT?

**T**he **variegated texture** and irregular, rounded shape of a **sea sponge** make it a "natural" choice for special-effects painting. A **synthetic sponge**, on the other hand, tends to apply a more uniform amount of paint and produces a more regular pattern and straight edges. In short, the synthetic sponge produces a manmade look, and the sea sponge a natural one.

# What to Buy

**1| PAINTER'S TAPE.** You'll need this tape to cover outlets and to mask off cabinets and the top of the backsplash.

**2| PINSTRIPING TAPE.** This thin masking tape is available at auto-supply stores. It's for masking off the grout lines. Tape that's ³/₁₆ in. wide is a good choice for this project.

**3| DISPOSABLE PLATES.** You'll need paper or plastic plates to mix up paint and glaze.

**4| ROLLER COVER.** To make quick work of applying the base coat, get a 9-in. roller cover with ³/₈-in. nap.

**5| BRUSHES.** You'll need a need a 2-in.- to 3-in.-wide nylon-polyester brush for cutting in and for applying varnish, an old natural-bristle brush for applying the tile paint, and an

artist's brush and toothbrush for some of the decorative tricks that add realism.

**6| SEA SPONGE.** Many faux finishers rely on this natural sponge to blend and mottle paint and glazes.

**7| PAINT & GLAZE.** Get three or more colors of acrylic-latex paint (eggshell sheen) that go with your kitchen décor. Small quantities (1 pint) are fine. For this project, we used white, gold, medium brown, and green. You'll also need water-based glaze, a clear medium that adds a transparency to the colors.

**8| LATEX GLOVES.** Sponge painting is messy work. Disposable latex gloves will help you keep your hands clean.

**9| CLEAR ACRYLIC FLOOR FINISH.** This super-durable varnish is the top coat that will make your faux tile nearly as stain-resistant as the real thing. Most brands will dry quickly, allowing you to apply several coats in the same day. Choose satin or gloss sheen.

**10| ACRYLIC-LATEX CAULK.** If you detect any gaps between the countertop backsplash and the wall, you'll need to fill these with caulk.

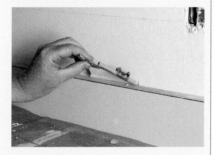
# Prepare To "Tile"

**1** **MASK & CAULK.** Apply masking tape as needed to protect the counter, backsplash, and cabinets. If there are any open cracks between the counter (or backsplash) and the wall, fill them with acrylic-latex caulk. Cut about ¼-in. off the tip of the cartridge (or tube) to open the caulk.

**2** **APPLY THE BASE COAT.** The paint should be the intended color of the "grout," with an eggshell sheen. Use a brush to cut in above the countertop and a roller to coat the rest of the backsplash area.

**3** **MARK HORIZONTAL GROUT LINES.** When the base coat has dried, measure the height of the tile area and determine a suitable tile size, such as 4x4, 4x6, or 5x5. Measure up from the countertop and mark the wall in several places to locate the horizontal grout lines. Use your level to check for horizontal, then lightly pencil a line about ³⁄₁₆-in. above each horizontal course line.

**4** **MARK VERTICAL GROUT LINES.** Measure the width of the tile area. Divide the result by the tile dimension plus the width of your pinstriping tape. (If the result produces too small a tile at one end, increase the width of the tiles a little.) Measure and mark the vertical grout lines as above, but this time pencil the line ³⁄₁₆-in. to the right of your mark each time.

**5** **TAPE YOUR GROUT LINES.** Apply the pinstriping tape just below the horizontal pencil lines and just to the left of the vertical ones. Then erase any pencil marks that are still visible so they don't show through the painted tiles.

**Putting three colors of paint** plus glaze on a single plate can get messy, especially when you're dipping in and out with the same brush. If you feel like you're losing control of the color combinations you want to apply, start with a fresh plate of paint. Or you might be more comfortable using separate plates for each color, and even separate brushes.

**▶ DO IT RIGHT**

**In an effort to fool the eye** and add to the illusion of depth, use an artist's brush and the dark glaze to paint a thin deep shadow line on one side and the bottom of each tile. Hold up your hand to see where a shadow naturally occurs.

# Paint the "Tiles"

**6** **DISH UP YOUR PAINT & GLAZE.** Pour a dollop of each color onto a plastic plate, along with a larger dollop of clear glaze. Apply the colors in succession to each tile, dabbing a nearly dry brush into a color, into the glaze, and then onto the wall. The more glaze you blend in, the more transparent the overall tile color will be. Now "smoosh" the colors together on the wall with a damp sponge. Give your wrist a slight twist to blend the colors together.

**7** **ADD DEPTH.** This step shades the perimeter of each tile to give depth to your backsplash. Mix three parts glaze to one part medium brown paint. Dip an old soft-bristle brush into the mixture, dab it nearly dry on paper towel, and then brush along the edge of each tile to add a soft shadow. For still more realism and depth, blend glaze and white paint together (about a 3:1 ratio) and brush this lightly over the centers of the tiles. This adds a soft highlight.

**8** **ADD TEXTURE, THEN TOSS THE TAPE.** If you want a limestone or handmade tile effect, dip the bristles of a toothbrush in paint and hold the brush a few inches away from the wall. Draw your thumb over the bristles to spatter. Not sure of your technique? Practice on newspaper first. When the paint dries, peel off and discard the tape.

**9** **SEAL THE TILES.** To make your tiles durable and easy to clean, apply several coats of clear acrylic floor finish with a varnish brush. Let the finish dry as directed between coats. Remove masking tape from outlets and replace the cover plates. You're done! It's time to invite a few friends over to see the expensive tile job you just completed.

**6 7**

**8 9**

The range of tile styles to imitate is limited only by your imagination. Grout lines can be thin or thick, grout can be white or not, and you can even paint on shadows.

# Creating faux tile effects is a bit like working with real tile:
It takes practice to grow confident in your technique. As you experiment with sample boards, paints, and various application techniques, you'll find that options are wide open for tile colors, patterns, and grout lines. After settling on a design, take the time to prepare the surface properly by masking, applying a base coat, and measuring grout lines carefully. And once you're done, protect your handiwork with a couple coats of clear acrylic finish.

Master the technique for faux tile and you're just a step away from turning a wood cornice molding into sculpted stone and transforming drywall surfaces into aged plaster.

Why stop at the wall? You can use the same faux painting technique to "install" tile along a windowsill and around the jamb.

# Subtle Stripes

Give any room an elegant, intriguing identity by using **TWO SHEENS** of a single color

NE COLOR AND TWO SHEENS. This simple recipe yields a striped wall that's subtle, upbeat, and elegant. It's a look that's great for a dining room, a study, or an entry foyer. Depending on the time of day and the light in the room, your view of a single hue changes, thanks to the difference between eggshell and semigloss. To work this magic on a wall in your house, you'll spend just as much time masking off the stripes as you will applying paint. Recruit a partner and you'll have no trouble striping a room in a weekend.

**EGGSHELL BASE COAT**  **STRIPE #1**  **PLENTY OF TAPE**  **TALE OF TWO SHEENS**

# Tools & Gear

**Not all painter's tape** is blue, and not all blue painter's tapes are the same. Although these tapes are all deigned for masking purposes, it's important to choose the tape's level of tack or sticking power carefully. Make sure to read the label, and consult with your paint dealer about the right tape to buy.

*In addition to your basic painting gear, you'll need a few tools for laying out the stripes and for prepping the walls.*

**TAPE MEASURE.** Get a 16-ft. or 25-ft. tape for measuring your walls and laying out your stripes.

**LEVELS.** You'll need a 4-ft. (or longer) level to mark vertical stripe lines. A small torpedo level will be helpful for making taping marks in tight spots—above windows, for example.

**BRUSH, ROLLERS, TRAYS & POLES.** You'll need this basic painting gear to apply the base coats and high-gloss stripes. For cutting in, you'll need a 3-in. or larger brush. Get a regular 9-in. roller (for base coats) and a 4-in. roller for painting the stripes. An extension pole will enable you to paint the top of the wall without getting on a ladder.

**DROP CLOTHS.** Protect your floors with canvas drop cloths rather than with plastic. Use a double drop cloth layer if the room has wall-to-wall carpeting.

**STEPLADDER OR STEPSTOOL.** There's lots of up-and-down work during layout, taping, and cutting in, so you'll need some sturdy steps that are easy to move around.

## COOL TOOL

**A**lthough you can use any ruler to make a scale drawing, you won't find a more useful drawing tool than an architect's scale. Triangular in section, this well-versed ruler contains nine different scales that range from $^3/_{32}$ in.= 1 ft. to 3 in. = 1 ft.

# What to Buy

**1 | DRAWING STUFF.** It's possible to use a drawing or design program on your computer to figure out the layout of your stripes. But if paper and pencil are more your style, get a drafting triangle for drawing straight lines and square corners. It's also good to have an architect's scale.

**2 | PAINT.** You want 100% acrylic-latex interior paint in two sheens: eggshell and high gloss. When calculating coverage, plan to apply two base coats and one or two coats for the high-gloss stripes.

**3 | ROLLER COVERS.** Get a ³/₈-in. or ¹/₂-in. nap roller cover for your 9-in. and 4-in. rollers.

**4 | PAINTER'S TAPE.** To mask the trim in your room, you'll need a single 1¹/₂-in. roll of medium-tack painter's tape. To mask off walls for striping, get two or three 60-yd. rolls of low-tack painter's tape in 2-in. width.

## PLANNING YOUR STRIPES

*There are many variations possible in painting stripes on a wall—width, color, sheen, and glazing treatments, for example. Here are some tips you can use to get great results no matter what striping scheme you go with.*

**1 |** Plan the pattern for the dominant wall first. This is usually the wall with a focal point, such as a fireplace or a pair of windows. The wall opposite the main entrance can also be the dominant wall.

**2 |** Locate a stripe adjacent to or straddling the centerline of the room or the focal point. But also pay attention to how stripes will align with the edges of the window and door trim.

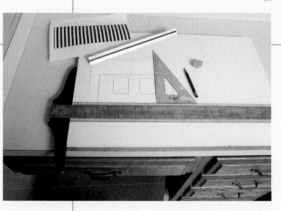

**3 |** Adjust stripe width as necessary. The wider the stripe, the more you can adjust without noticing. Make adjustments at corners or above windows and doors if possible.

**4 |** Wrap stripes around corners. If you're striping more than one wall, let your stripes wrap around corners. Keep in mind that corners present good opportunities for adjusting stripe width.

# Painting Stripes

**1** **APPLY THE BASE COAT.** Apply one or two coats of acrylic latex paint. For single-color stripes, apply the lower sheen paint first. Here the base is eggshell, and the stripes will be high gloss. Before you roll, cut in with a brush at the ceiling, along the baseboard, and around window and door trim. If you need to make any repairs or paint the ceiling or trim, do that work first (see Paint a Room, p. 22, and Painting Trim, p. 34). Allow the base coat to dry for at least 24 hours.

**2** **LOCATE THE FIRST STRIPE.** Find the center, mark 3 in. to either side, and use a 4-ft. level to tell you where the first strips of tape need to go. With the level held plumb, make light pencil marks at the top, middle, and bottom of the wall. Apply 2-in. painter's tape on the marks so that the tape masks the "not-to-be-painted" areas on either side of the first stripe. (For this project, we chose 6-in.-wide stripes and our dominant wall had two windows.)

**3** **MASK OFF STRIPES.** From the two vertical starting lines established in Step 2, measure, mark, and mask all other stripes on the wall. If there's any danger of confusing which strips of wall need to be painted, you can use a felt marker to write on your masking tape  or put extra tape to mark where not to paint (see the photo). As you apply each length of tape, make sure to burnish it down to prevent paint from bleeding under the tape (see DO IT RIGHT, left).

**4** **PAINT THE STRIPES.** Cut in with a brush at the top and bottom of the wall and around any trim or fixtures. Do the rest of your painting with a roller. As you complete each wall, slowly pull off the masking tape and inspect immediately for any spots where paint has bled under the tape. Wipe this bleed-through off with a damp paper towel. If the paint has already dried, razor it off (see WHAT CAN GO WRONG, left).

**1**

**2**

**3**

**4**

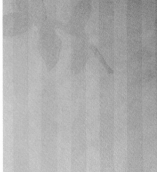

Stripes come in all thicknesses and directions depending on the look you want. Think thin, wide, vertical, horizontal—even diagonal.

If you think about it, these are really harlequin-shaped stripes—they just take a bit more planning and tape. After applying the pink base coat, the lighter diamonds were taped off and painted; later, the darker diamonds were painted. It's important to allow plenty of drying time before applying tape to fresh paint.

**If you master** the masking techniques necessary for striping a wall, there's a world of design options you can explore. Color and sheen differences can be subtle, dramatic, or anything in between. How about varying the size or spacing of your stripes, or forcing them to cross the wall at an angle instead of straight up and down? As you can see here, a little creativity will go a long way toward transforming a room with striping techniques.

One way to add interest to painted stripes is to use texturing techniques, as shown here.

Consider horizontal stripes to minimize the impact of tall, narrow doors or windows. Different tones of yellow and green create an optimistic atmosphere and counteract the formality of traditional molding details.

# Don't Forget the Floor

## Who needs a rug when you can create your own **PATTERN & COLOR** scheme with paint?

**T**ODAY, JUST ABOUT ANY WOOD FLOOR can gain a colorful new identity with decorative paint treatments that can be protected by durable, nonyellowing varnish. The floor featured here has a painted diamond-pattern "rug" with an optional stencil border. Instead of simply rolling on a second color, two colors were applied to alternate diamonds using decorative techniques called color-washing and ragging-off, creating a combination of hues and a textured effect. Floor painting takes a room out of commission for a few days, but it's a healthier, more up-to-date alternative to wall-to-wall carpeting. And it's a dramatic way to transform any room in your home.

| SAND THE FLOOR | BACKGROUND COLOR | MASK & PAINT | CLEAR FINISH |

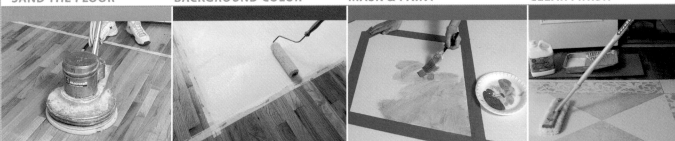

## ✚ WHAT CAN GO WRONG

**Even after scuff-sanding,** primer can have a tough time adhering to certain floor finishes, especially gloss polyurethane. For an extra measure of protection, apply a coat of deglosser just before you roll on the primer. Deglosser is available where paint is sold.

## ▶ DO IT RIGHT

**Before you begin** to paint a wood floor, see if any repairs need to be made. You can fill holes and gaps between boards with a suitable wood filler, available where paints and finishes are sold. Loose floor-boards can be screwed down with finishing screws, but make sure to countersink each screw below the wood surface and fill the recess.

# Tools & Gear

**RANDOM-ORBIT SANDER.** This portable electric sander and a good supply of 120-grit sanding discs will do a fine job of scuff-sanding the finish over a small area—up to around 8 ft. x 10 ft. To handle larger floor areas or simply get the job done faster, rent a floor polisher or hire a wood-flooring contractor.

**PAINT ROLLER & POLE.** Save your back when painting the floor by screwing an extension handle into your roller when applying the primer and base coat of paint.

**KNEE PADS.** Save your knees during sanding, layout, and taping by wearing these specially designed pads.

**TAPE MEASURE.** A 25-ft. tape with a broad (1-in.) width is a good bet for the measuring you need to do. The wider tape stays straight when extended along the floor.

**CHALK LINE & LONG STRAIGHTEDGE.** Use these to transfer your plan from paper to the floor.

## COOL TOOL

**A** **floor polisher** equipped with a fine (120-grit) abrasive screen is essential when scuff-sanding large floor areas. Most rental centers will let you rent one of these for half a day. Have your dealer demonstrate how to use it. At home, you can practice with the pad only (no screen) in a large open area until you get the knack.

# What to Buy

**1 | DISPOSABLE DUST MASK.** Don't go without this safety gear when sanding your floor.

**2 | PAINTER'S TAPE.** You'll need this low-tack tape for masking off the pattern of your painted "rug." Go with 2-in. width.

**3 | PRIMER.** Make sure to buy a top-quality primer compatible with the top coat. If your floor has a thick or shiny coat of varnish on it, consider treating this finish with a deglosser as well as a primer. (See WHAT CAN GO WRONG on the facing page.)

**4 | PAINT & GLAZE.** For the base coat, buy 100% acrylic-latex paint with an eggshell sheen. On this project, two premixed color glazes were used for the diamonds and surrounding stencil.

**5 | VARNISH.** Buy a top-quality water-based varnish to apply as a protective top coat over your paint and glaze.

**6 | LAMB'S WOOL APPLICATOR.** You'll need one of these or a big (4-in.) varnish brush to apply the varnish top coat.

**7 | ROLLER COVERS.** Have several roller covers on hand. Buy covers with a $\frac{3}{8}$-in. or $\frac{1}{2}$-in. nap.

**8 | FAUX APPLICATORS.** Rags, a natural sponge, and painter's plastic make good tools for blending and texturing glaze.

**9 | STENCILING SUPPLIES.** If you want to stencil a pattern around the edge of your painted rug (see Design Options, p. 118), buy a decorative pattern from a paint or craft supply store. You'll also need a stencil brush. For more details on stenciling, see p. 74.

**10 | PAINT PEN.** Used creatively, these pens can emphasize a pattern or cover small mistakes. They're available in different permanent colors from art supply stores.

## DESIGNING YOUR FLOOR

**There's no end** to the variety of "rugs" you can paint on your floor. For a few ideas, see the design options on p. 118. If you're going to paint a geometric pattern like the one shown here, try these tips for generating the final dimensions.

**1 | Plan it on paper first.** Graph paper makes it easy to draw room dimensions and test designs. Or you can use a computer drawing program.

**2 | Adjust outside dimensions to get the design right.** This enables you to avoid having partial or awkwardly sized shapes at the edges of your pattern. Keep in mind that one way to

increase the size of your design is to add a border outside a patterned interior.

**3 | Make use of centerlines.** Unless you are centering a design under a chandelier, as in this project, finding the center of the room will be your first step in laying out the design on the floor. It's easier to maintain alignment when pattern corners fall along the room's two centerlines.

**4 | Test for square with the 3-4-5 right triangle rule** (see the drawing at right). Measure 3 ft. from the corner on one side and 4 ft. on the other. Then measure the distance between those two points. If it's exactly 5 ft., you've got a square corner. If not, fine-tune the corner angle.

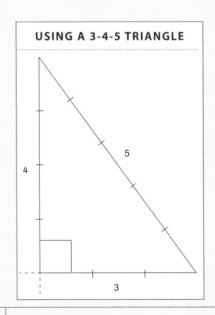

USING A 3-4-5 TRIANGLE

**A plumb bob** is nothing more than a heavy, pointed weight attached to a string. But this ancient layout tool is indispensable for pinpointing the location of one point exactly below another, in this case the center of a painted "rug" right below a chandelier.

**Paint can bleed** under masking tape if the tape isn't adequately adhered. To avoid irregular borders, burnish the edge of the tape after you press it in place with a pen or other smooth, hard object.

# Scuff, Tape & Paint

**1**   **LAYOUT & MASK OFF.** Locate the center of your floor painting by hanging a plumb bob from a chandelier, as done in this case, or by measuring off the walls to find the room center. Then use a chalk line or pencil and straightedge to mark two perpendicular centerlines that intersect at the center point. Measure from those lines to locate the outside dimensions of your rug and mask it off with tape.

**2**   **SCUFF-SAND.** Lightly sand the floor within the tape to remove all sheen using a floor polisher and a 120-grit screen. You can rent this equipment or have a floor refinishing pro do the work for you. For a small area, you can save money by sanding with a random-orbit sander and some 120-grit discs.

**3**   **REMOVE ALL DUST.** Vacuum up as much dust as possible, then go over the floor with a tack cloth or lint-free rag dampened with mineral spirits to remove the rest.

**4**   **ROLL ON PRIMER.** Use a paint roller and extension handle to apply a latex primer. When it is dry, apply two top coats of acrylic-latex paint in the base color you've chosen. Follow the manufacturer's instructions on drying time between coats.

❖ **COOL TOOL**

**A paint pen,** available in different colors from artist supply stores, is a great tool for putting a clean edge around the outside of your rug. It's also good for defining endpoints, emphasizing pattern lines, and covering mistakes with accent lines. You can use the pen freehand or guide it against a stencil or straightedge.

# Creating the Pattern

**5** **LAY OUT & MASK OFF FLOOR.** If necessary, repeat the technique in Step 1 to find the center of your floor. Then lightly pencil two centerlines that intersect at the center point. Transfer the design from your plan to the floor by measuring off both centerlines. When you've finished penciling in the pattern, mask it off with painter's tape.

**6** **APPLY YOUR COLOR(S).** You can complete a checkerboard floor with just two colors, but here we used a blend of glazes, mixed on a paper plate. Dab your brush into the glaze, then apply inside the tape. You can do this quickly; blending the glazes comes next.

**7** **ADD SOME TEXTURE.** It's time to "manipulate" the glaze and create some visual interest. Crumpled plastic makes a good texturing tool. Use a dab-and-twist motion. When your plastic gets too wet, replace it with a fresh piece. After the glaze dries, remove the painter's tape.

**8** **ADD ACCENT SQUARES & SEAL.** Small squares in a contrasting color add visual interest and also cover less-than-perfect corners where checkerboard lines converge. Mask each square off with painter's tape, then paint inside the taped area. Remove the tape after the paint dries, then protect your painted floor with several coats of clear floor finish. Looks great!

**5** **6**

**7** **8**

**To dress up your checkerboard floor, why not use a stencil to add a border.**

**There's no nicer way** to rescue an old wood floor than with a beautiful and distinctive paint job. And your design options are truly without limit. You can choose your pattern and colors and even add decorative touches, such as using stencils to create a border. Pull colors from the fabrics or other elements in the room. Paint the whole floor or just a faux rug. Remember: It's just paint!

When you're painting a checkerboard-type pattern, you can expect that your "tiles" won't all meet precisely point to point. To conceal any minor misalignment, try adding a small design at the point. It's a nice decorative touch that's worth considering even if the tile points are perfect. Dots in a contrasting color work well. So do painted or stenciled details. (See the photos at left.)

Don't stop with the floor. Window shutters, stencils, and a painted antique bureau are all part of this bedroom makeover.

Although you can simply brush another color paint on alternate tiles to create your floor pattern, easy-to-use decorative techniques and colored glaze generally give the floor a more interesting, textured appearance. *Combing* the glaze immediately after it is brushed on exposes the lighter base coat. When *stippling*, the glaze is applied with a stippling brush using a tapping motion.

# Photo Credits

All photos appearing in this book are © David Bravo, except:

p. 23: © Randy O'Rourke

p. 31: (left) Photo by Charles Bickford, courtesy *Fine Homebuilding,* © The Taunton Press, Inc.; (right) © Randy O'Rourke

p. 32: (left) Photo by Charles Bickford, courtesy *Fine Homebuilding,* © The Taunton Press, Inc.; © Dutch Boy

p. 33: (left) © Randy O'Rourke; (right) © davidduncanlivingston.com; (bottom) © Dutch Boy

p. 35: © Grey Crawford

p. 44: (left) © Pete Hecht/Mark Lisk Studio; (right) © Kerry Hayes

p. 45: (left) Photo by Charles Miller, courtesy *Fine Homebuilding,* © The Taunton Press, Inc.; (right) Photo by Andy Engel, courtesy *Fine Homebuilding,* © The Taunton Press, Inc.

p. 54: (bottom left) © Kitchens by Deane; (bottom right) © Randy O'Rourke

p. 55 (left) © Jason McConathy; (right) © Kitchens by Deane

p. 57: © Randy O'Rourke

p. 64: All photos © Randy O'Rourke

p. 65: All photos © Randy O'Rourke

p. 67: © Randy O'Rourke

p. 72: All photos © Randy O'Rourke

p. 73: © Randy O'Rourke

p. 75: © Randy O'Rourke

p. 82: (top) Photos provided by Stencil Planet. For more information, call 187-Stencil or visit www.stencilplanet.com; (bottom left and right) © Randy O'Rourke

p. 83: (top) Photos provided by Stencil Planet. For more information, call 187-Stencil or visit www.stencilplanet.com

p. 85: © Randy O'Rourke

p. 90: (left) © Andrew Bordwin; (right) © Roger Turk

p. 91: (top) © Steve Vierra Photography; (bottom) © davidduncanlivingston.com

p. 100: (left and right) © Randy O'Rourke

p. 101: (top and bottom) © Randy O'Rourke

p. 103: © Randy O'Rourke

p. 108: (bottom left corner and photo at right) © Randy O'Rourke

p. 109: (left) © Rohm + Haas; (top right) © Grey Crawford; (bottom right) © Randy O'Rourke

p. 118: (top right) © Randy O'Rourke

For more great weekend project ideas look for these and other
**TAUNTON PRESS BOOKS** wherever books are sold.

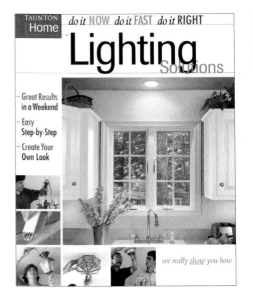

w.doitnowfastright.com